Praise for (

"If you have ever simply gone online, perhaps used social media or even just taken a picture with your smart phone, you likely have no idea about the obvious digital trail you have willingly left behind that others can follow to potentially use against you. Many different industries, from insurance and credit card companies, to employers, schools, and law enforcement already use this data to your disadvantage. And then there are the online bullies and predators preying on your kids. This is a truly remarkable must-read book. Finally, we have a clear and honest, behind-the-scenes guide for anyone who cares to protect the online personal and professional reputations of themselves and their children. The information in *Catching the Catfishers* is nothing short of astounding. Tyler Cohen Wood is a cyber security expert with Department of Defense credentials and is willing to share what she has learned. Thankfully her style is direct, understandable, and down-to-earth. One warning: At first you may be a little shocked or frightened as you read this book (frankly, you should be), but Ms. Wood offers many sound and practical steps you can take to protect yourself and your family. This book covers it all. We are even told how experts can tell when someone we are communicating with online is trying to lie and deceive us. It's a new world, and this manual should be in every home."

—Dr. Dean Edell, host, *Dr. Dean Edell Show*, author of *Life, Liberty, and the Pursuit of Healthiness*, and winner of many awards such as a national Emmy

Catching
the
Catfishers

Catching the Catfishers

Disarm the Online Pretenders,
Predators, and Perpetrators
Who Are Out to Ruin Your Life

Tyler Cohen Wood

CAREER
PRESS

The Career Press, Inc.
Pompton Plains, NJ

CATCHING THE CATFISHERS
EDITED BY KIRSTEN DALLEY
TYPESET BY GINA SCHENCK
Cover design by Rob Johnson
Printed in the U.S.A.

To order this title, please call toll-free 1-800-CAREER-1 (NJ and Canada: 201-848-0310) to order using VISA or MasterCard, or for further information on books from Career Press.

The Career Press, Inc.
220 West Parkway, Unit 12
Pompton Plains, NJ 07444
www.careerpress.com

Library of Congress Cataloging-in-Publication Data
Wood, Tyler Cohen, 1973-
 Catching the catfishers : disarm the online pretenders, predators, and perpetrators who are out to ruin your life / by Tyler Cohen Wood. -- 1 Edition.
     pages cm
 Includes bibliographical references and index.
 ISBN 978-1-60163-307-1 -- ISBN 978-1-60163-485-6 (ebook) 1. Online identity theft. 2. Online identity theft--Prevention. I. Title.

 HV6675.W66 2014
 613.60285'4678--dc23
                                                                    2013045967

Acknowledgments

Firstly, I'd like to thank Michael and Kirsten and all of Career Press for believing in me and this book.

I'd like to thank Donn for his help with all things lawyer; everyone who participated in my polls; AshleyGAGA and Rena Havey for their expertise in blogging; Paul and Sandy and the Woman and my father, for being the most supportive parents and in-laws anyone could ask for; and Courtney, George, Tracy, Brenna, Ryan, Zayne, Lissy, and all my other dear friends who wouldn't let me give up.

Most of all I want to thank my soul mate and husband, Matt, for being my rock and helping to make our dreams come true.

Contents

**Part II
Cyber Judo 101: Protecting Yourself and Your Family
From Predators, Liars, and Bullies**

Author's Note

All views are my own and do not reflect those of my employing agency or the United States government.

}-(((*>

Part I

Understanding the Online Domain

<0))))x

Controlling Your Online Persona

><((((o>

1

When I first met my coworker Charles (not his real name), it was like kismet. We both cared passionately about what we did for a living and how it affected the law enforcement, federal, and intelligence communities. Both of us were technically proficient and had many years of experience supporting federal law enforcement as digital forensic analysts. We became very close professionally. We collaborated on numerous projects and spent a great deal of time together. I knew that I could count on him for anything, and he knew the same was true about me. To me, Charles was a genuine and caring person who cared passionately about his work. A few months into our friendship and working relationship, however, I began hearing stories from other people who had worked with both of us on separate projects that he was arrogant and not a team player. I dismissed these stories as gossip. I "knew" Charles. There was no way that the person

I knew and had worked closely with for a year was arrogant or rude, or didn't work well with others. *They just don't know him*, I thought. A year into working with Charles, we became friends on various social media sites. I began to follow his blog and Facebook posts. After just two weeks of following him on social media, I began to see a very different side of Charles. He was extremely condescending in his posts and comments to other people, and put them down, often harshly, with very little provocation. He was arrogant and argumentative over minor things such as predicting the weather. I was completely shocked. I knew Charles. I had worked closely with him for a year. I had a very distinct perception of him, but there he was right in front of me, showing a completely different side of his personality. The person I saw was not at all the person I thought I knew. At first, I thought long and hard about which was the real Charles, but then I realized that it didn't matter. This arrogant online identity completely overshadowed the Charles I thought I knew. Perhaps predictably, our working relationship suffered. I no longer sought him out as an expert, and we eventually went our separate ways.

There is a saying that people tell the truth when they are drunk. The same can often be said for people when it comes to their online presence. Piecing together an online persona, if done correctly, can often yield a much more realistic impression of who a person is, better, even, than spending time getting to know him or her in person. Many (but not all) people tend to be much more honest and open about their innermost thoughts and feelings when they are online. Perhaps this is due to the fact that they feel anonymous and therefore protected behind their computer screens or mobile devices. Regardless of the reason, you will discover how to piece together the real person behind the online identity, as well as how to control the pieces of your own online identity to portray yourself in the best light possible.

We live in two worlds, and both are very real. One is the physical world that we have always lived in and are comfortable with. The other is the virtual world in which we create— sometimes inadvertently—our online identities and personas. These digital identities are just as integral a part of our daily lives as our identities are in the physical world.

Your online identity and persona can reveal a very detailed picture of who you are: your likes, your dislikes, your political views, your religious affiliation, your hobbies, and whom you associate with. Unless someone is deliberately manipulating it and disseminating untruths (more on this later in the book), a person's online persona is often more "real"—more authentic—than the persona he or she presents to the everyday world. In about an hour, I could learn virtually everything there is to know about you, simply by putting together all the disparate pieces of your online profile. Does this surprise you?

When I would conduct a digital forensic examination for a major crimes case, typically I would research the social media cache on a suspect's computer and investigate his online presence. Depending on the information that was "out there," within an hour I could put together a highly detailed profile of the person. I would know where he liked to go, what restaurants or bars he frequented, who his friends were, his posting style, his personality, as well as more intimate details about his life including his hobbies and dreams, information about his children, and the list goes on. I got to know these people in such detail that I felt as if I had indeed known them all my life. But this is not just a skill for someone who works in computer forensics; anyone can learn do this. You can learn how to read an online identity and put together all the digital puzzle pieces. Of course, this cuts both ways: Others out there can also discover all the puzzle pieces of your online identity. The good news is that you have absolute control over what and how you post and, therefore, how people will perceive you online.

The Components of Your Online Identity

Law enforcement can piece together a suspect or witness profile based on various elements of his or her online identity. The same elements comprise your online identity. You have communities that you post in or follow, such as blogs, forums, Facebook, and Twitter. These communities link you to other people. If you have friends who could be viewed as unsavory, you can be labeled the same way. It is the "birds of a feather, flock together" concept, which means that you are probably similar to the people you choose to associate with. Based on what you post and which blogs and sites you follow, your pattern of online behavior can easily be established. Law enforcement can establish your political views, your personal interests, whether you drink too much or not at all, and whether you are easily agitated and like to bully others online. (We will go into much more detail on behavior later.) Then there are the easily accessible online records that contain personal information such as addresses, criminal and financial records, credit reports, and schools or universities you attended. Using these three elements—communities, behavior, and records— a law enforcement official, a forensic analyst, a commercial predictive advertising company, or anyone with sufficient interest can look for consistencies, patterns, and anomalies in your online identity. With these elements, a life pattern or unique signature of the real person—you—emerges behind the online identity. Obviously, you have little control over credit reports or public records, but you do have complete control over what you choose to post, Tweet, or blog about.

First steps

It is important that you do a search of yourself online to see what others see when they search you. Try to do this with an unbiased opinion. It might make sense to you that you post your political views very passionately, but try to read what you have posted from the perspective of someone who may not agree with you and consider how they would view you. Might they find that your views are so passionately posted that they could perceive of you as a troublemaker and not want to hire you? Could those pictures from that bachelorette party come back to haunt you later? Use search engines to look yourself up. Search for your e-mail addresses, phone numbers, full name, avatars, or nicknames. You want to know what others will see and what perception of you they will put together. Again, think of it in terms of communities, behavior, and records. So, what if you find something that you don't want others to see? We will cover how to clean your online identity in later chapters but for now, take active steps to start thinking about how each thing that you post is a digital puzzle piece that, when put together, creates a detailed image of who you are.

The Rules of Engagement Are the Same

One of the most important points that you will learn throughout this book is that you want to behave online the same way you behave in the real world. Your online identity is instantly accessible to people all over the world who will make snap perceptions about you based on how your present yourself, just as they do in the physical world. Let's say I walked into a room as an expert on cyber topics, wearing a crop-top shirt and a miniskirt, to give a briefing to a senior official. Let's say I started my briefing by saying, "Ohmygod I am sooooo excited! This presentation is going to be totes amazeballs!" The senior official would automatically write me off as a joke, no matter how knowledgeable I was about my topic. It works the same in the online world. If I am always posting content that makes me appear immature, that is the perception people will have of me. If I walked into my boss's office and told him that I was sick of my job and thought he was an idiot, or if I showed him a photo of myself at Arlington National Cemetery flipping off the Tomb of the Unknown Soldier (like the photo that Lindsey Stone posted on her Facebook page[1]), I would be perceived as disrespectful and would probably get fired. Most people would never do this in real life, so why do it online? There is no difference. Again, people will perceive the "you" of your your online identity the same way they will perceive the "real you." If anything, you have to be more cautious about how you are perceived online because once it's out there for everyone to see, it's incredibly difficult to remove.

Your Legal Rights

Laws governing social media are being debated and created each and every day, through policy and cases. There are privacy laws that dictate who owns your online content, and whether your words are protected by free speech when you are operating in the online domain. According to *Social Media and the Law: A Guidebook for Communication Studies*:

> If a social media user posts information to their profile, can I assume that it is not private information and thus free to use?
>
> There is no categorically absolute answer to this question. Context, the nature of the information, the role of the user and your relationship with that user, the privacy settings, and any other implied and explicit terms of disclosure are all relevant in determining if information shared within a social network site can be appropriately shared of used elsewhere.[2]

Essentially, in layperson's terms, the answer to this question is, it depends. The crux of the issue is whether or not a person has a reasonable expectation of privacy regarding self-disclosed information, as well as who actually owns said posted content. Should we really have any expectation of privacy to self-disclosed content that we have selectively and voluntarily chosen to post on social media?

If I walked into a room of friends and gave each of them a copy of a photograph of me doing something inappropriate, do I still own that photograph or have any ability to control what my friends do with it? What expectation of privacy do

I have with regard to that photograph? I am not a lawyer, but logic dictates that because I have given it to everyone in that room, they can do anything they want with it: pass it along to others, post it on a billboard—you get the idea. It is my personal opinion that posting anything to social media is the same as physically giving it out to people, and that you no longer have the ability to control what they do with that content in its original form. (An exception: If they change the content and use the changed content in a defamatory manner against you, that is a different story. We will discuss that in Chapter 7.)

There is a widely held misconception that we are protected by privacy settings on social media sites. However, the terms of service (TOS) that you agreed to when you signed up in order to use a service such as Facebook is actually a contract between you and the social media site. I have read through the terms of service for a few of the social media sites and they very explicitly state in relatively non-legalese (clear English) what rights they have to your content, what information they can collect on you, and what they can do with that information. They also state very clearly that their privacy policy can change at any time.

> *On October 10, 2013, Facebook changed its privacy policy and removed a setting allowing users' timelines to be hidden from public searches. Thus, as of this writing, user timelines are searchable and viewable by anyone searching for them by name.*

According to the Facebook Statement of Rights and Responsibilities:

You own all of the content and information you post on Facebook, and you can control how it is shared through your privacy and application settings. In addition:

1. For content that is covered by intellectual property rights, like photos and videos (IP content), you specifically give us the following permission, subject to your privacy and application settings: you grant us a non-exclusive, transferable, sub-licensable, royalty-free, worldwide license to use any IP content that you post on or in connection with Facebook (IP License). This IP License ends when you delete your IP content or your account unless your content has been shared with others, and they have not deleted it....

4. When you publish content or information using the Public setting, it means that you are allowing everyone, including people off of Facebook, to access and use that information, and to associate it with you (i.e., your name and profile picture).[3]

When you agree to use Facebook, you are giving Facebook rights to your content. Even though it says that you own it, by posting it you are giving it a license to use the content. The worldwide license is also transferable to whomever Facebook chooses, meaning it can sell your data to whomever it wishes.

Nowhere in the TOS for Facebook (last revision date December 11, 2012) does it state that the people that you have chosen to share your content with do not have the right to reproduce and redistribute your content. In fact, according to item 4, quoted previously, if you use a "public" privacy setting on your content, you are allowing others to use your content and associate that content with you. There is much legal debate as to whether content posted to social media is copyrighted by the original creator. It depends on how the creator/writer has shared it (whom he or she has shared it with and what privacy settings), what the content is, and whether monetary value can be placed on the content (for example, if it is reproduced by a news organization or anyone else who then makes money off it). The lawyers can debate until they are blue in the face, and they probably will—the bottom line is, to protect yourself, it is best to not post anything that you would not want shared with the world.

> On April 29th 2013, University of Georgia freshman Chelsea Chaney filed a lawsuit against the Fayette County Public School District in Georgia, claiming that school officials used an image in an Internet safety presentation that they used from her Facebook page without her permission. They used the photo of her in a bikini with a caption of "Once It's There—It's There To Stay," implying that it was inappropriate to post the photo on Facebook.[4]

The outcome of this case could help determine who owns original content when it's posted to social media.

The news is full of stories of people getting fired over things they've posted on social media. For example:

> Lindsey Stone, a Plymouth, Massachusetts woman who posted a photo of herself giving the middle finger in front of the Tomb of the Unknown Soldier,

creating a firestorm of Internet backlash and outrage, lost her job Wednesday.

Stone's employer, Living Independently Forever, Inc., a non-profit based in Hyannis, announced that both Stone and the co-worker who took the photo were no longer working at the non-profit after thousands of people rallied for the pair to be removed from their jobs, saying what they did was disrespectful and offensive.[5]

The First Amendment states that "Congress shall make no law respecting an establishment of religion, or prohibiting the free exercise thereof; or abridging the freedom of speech, or of the press; or the right of the people peaceably to assemble, and to petition the government for a redress of grievances."[6] The First Amendment (the right to free speech) does not necessarily protect your "free speech" from the private sector. If you work for the private sector, you are most likely an "at-will" employee, meaning that it is at the company's discretion whether or not to take disciplinary action against you for anything that you say or that you post online.

Regardless of whether or not you think that this is right or wrong or an invasion of privacy, if you are an at-will employee of the private sector, a private employer has the right to fire you or not hire you for anything that you have posted or any information discovered about you online. That said, not all social media content is created equal. For example, it is much more difficult to determine whether something as seemingly innocuous as "liking" something on Facebook could be considered cause for termination. According to the book *Social Media and the Law: A Guidebook for Communication Students*:

A Hampton, Virginia sheriff fired six employees who supported an opposing candidate during his re-election campaign. One of the workers contended in federal court that he was fired for expressing his support of the other candidate by "liking" him on Facebook. The district court judge in this case ruled that the firing could not be linked to the employee's support of the opposition candidate because clicking the "like" button on Facebook was not equivalent to writing a message of support for the opposition candidate. The "like" button, the court found, was not expressive speech.[7]

We will probably see more and more cases involving the "like" button and whether it can be considered expressive speech in years to come. That said, be watchful of what you choose to "like." Remember that you want to control the perception that others have of you through your online identity. What you choose to "like" can tell people a lot about you! For example, if you want to keep your politics to yourself and take careful precautions not to post content discussing your political or social views on hot topics, yet always "like" when others post about particular issues, others will assume that you, too, share those views.

Most of us can apply common sense and know that posting something that is obviously illegal can get us arrested. But sometimes even posting a joke can get us into legal trouble. Richard Godbehere posted a self-made video called "Let's Go Driving, Drinking!" to LiveLeak, a video-sharing social media site. In the video, Godbehere appears to be driving his car. While driving, he opens a bottle of what appears to be beer and says he likes to drink German beers as he takes swigs from the bottle. He slurs his words and definitely appears drunk. The video goes on for exactly five minutes and 11 seconds. Although Godbehere claims that he was acting and that there was no beer in the bottle he was arrested for drinking and driving. According to a quote in a CNN story, "'In criminal cases, almost all evidence is discoverable and police can obtain the evidence,' said Bradley Shear, a Washington-area lawyer specializing in social media law. 'It's just a matter of what hoops they have to jump through.'"[8]

In following chapters I will go into greater detail on how to control your online identity, as well as how to piece together the pieces of other people's online identities. Always remember that you have ultimate control over what you choose to put online. It is also important to remember that the legal ground of social media is being determined as we speak, so use common sense and remember that posting online is not that different from how you ought to act in the physical world.

}-(((*⌐

A Little Privacy, Please

<0)))))x

Social media and our online activities connect us in ways that we could never have imagined previously. We have access to information instantly—whether we want to know everything about our favorite Hollywood star, keep track of emergencies or natural disasters as they unfold, follow experts in our industry, or simply keep in touch with family and friends. With the massive amounts of information that can be gleaned about someone simply by piecing together the digital "bread crumb trail" each one of us leaves behind (whether we know it or not), we have access to the daily lives and innermost thoughts of people we don't even know.

As I discussed in the previous chapter, many people believe (erroneously) that they are protected by privacy settings on social media sites. This false sense of security can encourage people to post things that they wouldn't say in person. There is also a false sense of anonymity when we are online because we are not physically in front of people. This sense of anonymity is boosted when people use a fake e-mail address or an anonymous proxy server (a sort of digital mask for your identifying information) or avatar. From my years as a computer forensic examiner, I know that you are not nearly as anonymous as you might think. You will almost always leave a digital trail of crumbs behind you wherever you go online, and with predictive data analytics software becoming more prevalent and more powerful, if someone really wants to find you or know your business, they almost always will.

Another thing to keep in mind is that privacy settings on applications and social media sites can change in a heartbeat, giving the companies whose software or networks that you use full access to your data. Remember, the company whose software you are using is out to make money with your data and does not necessarily have any interest in protecting your privacy. In fact, when you clicked that you read the terms of service and agreed to use their site or application, you probably signed a contract allowing the company access and perhaps even rights to your content. Some people get upset over this and feel that it's an invasion of privacy. They don't think that companies should be allowed to track their every move and build a digital personality profile on them. However, understand that it is not an invasion of your privacy because you are choosing not only to use their services but also what to put out there. *You have full control over what you post.* Think about how much easier our lives have become now that virtually everyone has a personal computer, smartphone, or tablet with them at all times. We may not like that companies track us when we use their software or applications, but remember, we are choosing to use them. I can't live without the GPS navigation program on my phone. I know that most applications (apps) track my movements. In fact, it can be argued that to be able to use most of the services that we have come to rely on, we have to give up some privacy. For example, location service–based applications simply won't work if you don't allow the application access to your location and GPS coordinates.

The Digital Puzzle Pieces of Your Life

Each time you post something to a blog or social media site, you are posting a digital puzzle piece. Each post by itself may seem innocuous, but when all the digital puzzle pieces are put together, the result paints a picture of who you are to advertisers, potential employers, other professionals, and even potential dates. Each piece by itself might not say much about you—whether it is location data, a posting to a friend, a "like" for a friend's posting about his or her political views, or a picture of something important to you—but when the pieces are put together, a spookily accurate portrayal can emerge of who you are as a person. It is important to control these digital puzzle pieces so that when put together, they align with person you present to the world. Whether they are using software or manually putting together all the disparate pieces, it is all too easy for anyone to find out who you *really* are.

In later chapters we will evaluate how to take control of the digital puzzle pieces or breadcrumbs (pick the metaphor that works for you!) that you leave behind so that you can paint the picture you want others to see. First, however, it is important to know what some of these digital puzzle pieces are, and to understand that you might be leaving behind some pretty revealing and intimate or confidential information in your wake. The first step is to understand who has access to your information and what information they have access to.

What everyone has access to

There are many social media aggregators, such as mylife. com or Spokeo.com (an open source social media portal) that will scour the entire Internet and piece together all of a person's digital puzzle pieces and put them together in one report for anyone to view. You can run searches using nothing more than a user name or e-mail address. The average person also has access to your social media (which can include location data), and can use the information therein to paint a picture of who you are and what your life is like. We will go into greater detail on this in the technical section of this chapter.

What commercial companies collecting your data have access to

If you read through the terms of service from the social media, Websites, and applications you use, they are usually pretty good about telling you exactly what they collect and what they do with that information. For example, Facebook's Terms of Service includes a Data Use Policy that you contractually agree to when to use their service. Facebook's Data Use Policy is very easy to read. From Facebook's Data Use Policy (last updated December 2011):

> We receive a number of different types of information about you, including:
>
> - Registration information.

- When you sign up for Facebook, you are required to provide information such as your name, email address, birthday, and gender. In some cases, you may be able to register using other information, like your telephone number.

- Information you choose to share.

- Your information also includes the information you choose to share on Facebook, such as when you post a status update, upload a photo, or comment on a friend's story.

- It also includes the information you choose to share when you take an action, such as when you add a friend, like a Page or a website, add a place to your story, use our contact importers, or indicate you are in a relationship.

Your name, profile pictures, cover photos, gender, networks, username and User ID are treated just like information you choose to make public. Your birthday allows us to do things like show you age-appropriate content and advertisements. We receive information about you from your friends and others, such as when they upload your contact information, post a photo of you, tag you in a photo or status update, or at a location, or add you to a group. When people use Facebook, they may store and share information about you and others that they have, such as when they upload and manage their invites and contacts. We also receive other types of information about you:

- We receive data about you whenever you interact with Facebook, such as when you look at another person's timeline, send or receive a message, search for a friend or a Page, click on, view or otherwise interact with things, use a Facebook mobile app, or purchase Facebook Credits or make other purchases through Facebook.

- When you post things like photos or videos on Facebook, we may receive additional related data (or metadata), such as the time, date, and place you took the photo or video.

- We receive data from the computer, mobile phone or other device you use to access Facebook, including when multiple users log in from the same device. This may include your IP address and other information about things like your internet service, location, the type (including identifiers) of browser you use, or the pages you visit. For example, we may get your GPS or other location information so we can tell you if any of your friends are nearby.

- We receive data whenever you visit a game, application, or website that uses Facebook Platform or visit a site with a Facebook feature (such as a social plugin), sometimes through cookies. This may include the date and time you visit the site; the web address, or URL, you're on; technical information about the IP address, browser and the operating system you use; and, if you are logged in to Facebook, your User ID.

- Sometimes we get data from our affiliates or our advertising partners, customers and other third parties that helps us (or them) deliver ads, understand online activity, and generally make Facebook better. For example, an advertiser may tell us information about you (like how you responded to an ad on Facebook or on another site) in order to measure the effectiveness of—and improve the quality of—ads.

We also put together data from the information we already have about you and your friends. For example, we may put together data about you to determine which friends we should show you in your News Feed or suggest you tag in the photos you post. We may put together your current city with GPS and other location information we have about you to, for example, tell you and your friends about people or events nearby, or offer deals to you that you might be interested in. We may also put together data about you to serve you ads that might be more relevant to you.

When we get your GPS location, we put it together with other location information we have about you (like your current city). But we only keep it until it is no longer useful to provide you services, like keeping your last GPS coordinates to send you relevant notifications.[1]

As you can see, Facebook clearly states that they collect massive amounts of information about you and your devices to help link you to friends and target advertising so that you can better avail yourself of the perks of their service. It should come as no surprise that they have the ability to put together a very accurate portrayal of who you are as a person, because they tell you that they are you doing it, right there in black and white!

With Google Cards, which is available on Android devices, Google collects information from all of your Google applications, such as e-mail and maps, and uses this information to help you keep track of meetings and appointments. For example, my husband, Matt, uses Google Cards on his phone. Recently, he had used his Gmail account to accept an invitation to a party. The address of the party was contained in the e-mail. Based on his Google Maps usage, Google knows where he lives and, using the geocoordinates on his phone, where he is at any point in time. Without him even having to do anything, the morning of the party, his Google Cards alerted him that based on his home address, the address of the party from the original e-mail, and the current traffic, we would have to leave by 10:30 to make it to the party on time. It had also found us an alternate route that would save us time and help avoid the traffic. What a fantastic service for those of us who tend to be forgetful! However, think about the massive amount of information that Google has collected on Matt through his Google services. Does it really matter that Google has all of that information about him? It depends. In its terms of service, stated in plain, easy-to-read English, Google tells you that it has the rights to that data and the ability to sell that data to other parties. I'm not here to say whether I think that giving up privacy to commercial companies and their ability to sell individuals' data is good or bad because, frankly, I feel it has both pros and cons. The point here is to make you aware of it so that you can have enough information to make your own decisions on whether or not you want to use these services.

In order to have that easy and instant access to information that most of us have come to expect, you have to give up some privacy. No longer can we protect our privacy 100 percent. Later in this chapter, I will delve into more technical details, showing how companies whose software you use collect data on you and how to protect yourself from this as much as possible. Remember that the best protection is knowledge of how things work, and if you don't want something known, don't put it out there. Assume that everything you post and everywhere you take your phone is discoverable, and use that knowledge to your advantage.

Potential or current friends or romantic partners Google each other so frequently that "Google" is now an actual verb in the English language. But how many of us know that insurance companies are now using your online profiles to determine whether or not to insure you and what rates to charge you? Are there pictures of you online smoking and drinking? Are there pictures of you engaging in risky or dangerous behavior? Are you friends with people who engage in what an insurance company might deem risky behavior?

Credit card companies and banks are also investigating your online identities to see what you like to spend money on. Do you frequently talk about your expensive purchases that you can't really afford? Understand that credit card companies know whether or not you can afford something because they have your credit history. They know how much you make and they know how much your spouse makes, meaning they know what your household income is. Are you living beyond your means? Do you post anything or belong to sites that might make you appear to be risky to loan money to? Do you complain online about never having enough money? Do you have social media friends with bad credit? Remember, you are judged not only on your online identity but by the friends you keep online. Just read the following extract from a recent article in *Newsweek*:

> In 2009, a Quebec woman who was receiving sick leave for depression had her disability benefits revoked after her insurance company discovered photos on Facebook—her profile was public—where she looked like she was having fun.... Credit-card companies use social media to determine what kind of offers might work the best on your social group—or to get insight on whether you'd default on a loan.[2]

It is not just targeted marketers that are interested in collecting your information. Most companies whose products you use and sites you visit, including cell phone manufacturers, wireless providers, and ISPs, have the ability to keep track of you and can and do sell that information to other parties.

Legal authorities and what they can access

If a computer, device, Website, app, ISP, or cloud server may contain potential evidence of a crime, legal authorities can get a warrant or consent to collect or search the information stored there. Data that is contained on a suspect's computer or digital device tends to be easiest to access. If suspected evidence is elsewhere, such as on an ISP, social media site's servers, or some other online storage, the data might not be as well-preserved; it may have even been deleted due to laws and/or the company's policy for storing records, which is why law enforcement will typically send a preservation letter to the service provider to keep all information related to an account.

Law enforcement professionals also use the Internet to create profiles of witnesses and suspects or to assist in tracking someone's movements. When I was a forensic examiner, I was involved in a case in which a potential suspect was accused of allegedly downloading and sharing child pornography (photographs and videos). The potential suspect was very careful to delete all traces of his activities using a wiping program. He used a fake name to sign up for a Web-based e-mail account, which he then linked to a fake mailing address. When surfing unsavory Websites or uploading photographs, he used proxy servers, which are servers that hide identifying information, such as your IP address, from the service provider you are going to. In this example, think of an IP address as a personal identifier when surfing or posting. By using a proxy server, he was using what he thoughts was an anonymous IP address that identified him as someone else in the logs of the Website he was surfing and to the routers that his traffic had to traverse to get to his destination Website. It would be similar to introducing yourself to strangers as someone else. He was very careful to wipe out all traces of his online activity from his computer. However, what he failed to take into account was that the proxy server kept logs of his real IP address; the server was also located within the United

States, which made it easy for the detective to get a warrant and send a preservation letter to the proxy service. When he created his fake e-mail accounts, he failed to use a proxy server, thus revealing his real identity to the Web mail server. He didn't use a proxy server when he was surfing and posting to unsavory sites using his smartphone, either. Finally, he tended to use a particular name and avatar no matter where he was on the Web. For example, his fake e-mail account included the name "X." He would use this name to post to his unsavory sites, yet he used the same name to post on other blogs and Websites such as CNN.com, and with his real IP address, too. He was very careful to clean his browser cache and history, and, as I mentioned, he used wiping programs to clean the unsavory photos and videos from his computer. He also deleted all the images from his smart phone. However, he didn't remove the photos from his smart-phone backups on his computer, and he failed to remove his history from Real Player (which he used to view his videos). He failed to clean his tracks in the registry keys, which allowed me to get an all-too-detailed picture of his activities. These are only a few of the things that he failed to do in order to make his actions undetectable. Throughout his activities he was leaving a trail of digital puzzle pieces that, when pieced together, created a very detailed picture of his involvement in illegal activities. I cannot discuss how the case ended, but I can say that he learned the hard way that you are not nearly as anonymous on the Internet as you think, and that it is practically impossible to remove all traces of your activities.

Law enforcement uses social media to catch criminals, often in sting operations. In 2006, I presented a forensic briefing at a California District Attorneys' conference. At that time social media had just started to go mainstream. One of the DAs I met at the conference told me a story about how social media helped him catch a criminal. The police had a hunch that a suspect had conducted a string of burglaries. No matter what they did, they couldn't get him to confess, and they didn't have enough evidence to hold him. They looked at his MySpace page and found nothing incriminating. However, one of the young detectives suggested that they also search his girlfriend's MySpace page. The suspect's girlfriend was so proud of her man that she had happily posted pictures of her "sexy bad boyfriend" holding some of the stolen items. You can guess how that ended when the suspect was confronted and shown the evidence against him.

Law enforcement and commercial companies have some very powerful social media aggregator software that they use to get a clearer picture of someone's presence online. Some companies are developing or already have tools that can use behavior analytics to help link together different social identities to determine if they are from the same person or multiple people hiding behind one identity. These are amazing and helpful tools. By analyzing patterns of behavior, writing styles, word usage, grammar, and so forth, they isolate any anomalies, thereby determining if there are multiple people posting to an account that is supposed to be one particular person, or uniquely identifying someone's signature even if the person is using tools to hide that signature.

How Does It Work? Predictive Analytics

A good friend of mine had a baby. I had no idea what to get her so I began searching online for ideas on what to get a new mother for her baby. I got distracted and began reading all kinds of blogs and articles about babies. I then asked my friends on a social media site what to get a new mother for her baby. The next time I logged into my Web-based e-mail account (which of course is attached to the search engine and the social media site I had used previously), I had several advertisements for products related to babies in my inbox. I am sure that most of you reading this book have had similar experiences. This is an example of targeted marketing based on predictive analysis. A friend of mine works for a targeted marketing company. When I asked him about this topic for this book, he told me that his company was so good at gathering data on people and piecing it together that if I were to give them an e-mail address, he would most likely be able to tell me the person's real name, address, how much they make, where they work, who their friends are, their spouses and children's names, and what their hobbies are. He said that his company could predict with a high percent of accuracy when and where this person would take their next vacation, what kind of car they were going to purchase next and when, what their next purchase would be, and where they were likely to be on any given day and time. Targeted marketing and predictive analysis through social media is big business, and your information and pattern of life are worth a lot of money. Advertisers have gotten smart and learned to capitalize on this.

Most people stick to a pattern of life that is easy to predict, once you know about it. It is easy to determine where you live, where you work, what restaurants you go to, who your friends are, who your partner is, whether you have children, what activities you engage in, your interests, and what you like to buy. Think about your life: Even though you are probably a busy person and feel as though you are always on the go and doing different things, you probably have a pretty routine life that follows a predictable pattern. Predictive analysis is an association of mixed protocols and applications that help advertisers and other companies put together a unique identifying signature, or pattern of life, on *you*.

HTML 5

The advent and use of HTML 5 and location-aware browsing have helped enhance predicative analysis and made it incredibly accurate. HTML 5 can tie your browsers to a location. Even though the following paragraph discusses Firefox, almost all browsers support location-aware browsing and HTML 5:

Websites that use location-aware browsing will ask where you are in order to bring you more relevant information, or to save you time while searching. Let's say you're looking for a pizza restaurant in your area. A website will be able to ask you to share your location so that simply searching for "pizza" will bring you the answers you need...no further information or extra typing required. If you consent, Firefox gathers information about nearby wireless access points and your computer's IP address. Then Firefox sends this information to the default geolocation service provider, Google Location Services, to get an estimate of your location. That location estimate is then shared with the requesting website. Firefox only requests a location when a website makes a request, and only shares your location when the user has approved the request. Firefox does not track or remember your location as you browse.[3]

For example, ads can be picked just for you, such as a restaurant suggestion based on your current location. The GEO cords are pulled right out of the browser, so it doesn't matter if you are on a laptop or a smart phone. Whatever Website you are visiting or whatever ISP you are using, "they" can easily pull your location data.

Location services

With every post you make to social media, you are leaving a digital breadcrumb or puzzle piece for someone to follow or piece together. Some social media sites allow you to "check in," thereby posting your GEO coordinates or location information. To really understand this concept, we have to discuss the location service that is used by Websites you visit or the applications (apps) on your phone that determine where you are and allow you to use navigation programs, check into places on Facebook or other social media, or find something close to your current location. Location-based services use information from cellular and GPS networks to determine your estimated location. Most of you have probably noticed that when you install your apps, you get a message on your phone asking you if it is okay to allow that app to use your location data. For an example, I have a Starbucks locator app on my phone that I use when I am in an unfamiliar area and have an emergency Starbucks craving. I have allowed the app to access my location data so that it can tell me where I can find the nearest Starbucks based on my approximate location. I have also allowed Facebook and other social media access to my location services so that people know where I am when I post something. Several dating services, such as SinglesAroundMe or Match.com, have apps that are based on the location service location app. Both of these sites use your location service to determine your exact location and let you know if someone who might be a good fit lives nearby. You can then chat with each other and meet up if you choose to.

EXIF data

The other concept we need to discuss is EXIF data. EXIF data stands for Exchangeable Image File and is the metadata captured by your camera. Most phone cameras or digital cameras have EXIF data turned on by default. If EXIF data is turned on, when you take a photograph, the EXIF data comes along with the photograph, but we can't see it unless we use special tools, most of which are free and available to anyone on the Internet. EXIF data contains information about the photograph such as where the photograph was taken (with exact GEO coordinates), what camera (including its serial number) took the photo, and many other details that give away information about you.

In 2012 a Burger King employee in Mayfield Heights, Ohio, posted a photograph of someone stepping in a tub of lettuce with their shoes on, with the caption, "This is the lettuce you eat at Burger King," to the Website 4chan.com, an image-based social media site where users can post pictures and make comments. The posters thought that they were anonymous because they showed no identifying details in the photo—or so they thought. The photograph contained EXIF data and GEO coordinates, so furious users were able to track down the exact Burger King where the photo had been taken. Once the local media was contacted, the three workers responsible for taking and posting the photograph were identified and quickly fired.[4]

Cookies

Cookies also collect information about you. A cookie is information placed on your device by an app or Website that keeps track of information about you, such as your e-mail address, what you search for and buy, or information unique to the device you are using to enhance data correlation. Some companies use software to read other companies' cookies to gather even more information about you. The software looks for what you have been searching for or buying as well as your e-mail address so that ads from that company can be targeted to you. These are called supercookies, Flash cookies, and/or zombie cookies. These supercookies are not kept in the same location on your device as regular cookies, which makes them hard to find and remove. Even if you regularly use your browser's function to remove cookies, browser removal will not work. As Ebezine.com claims:

> The new Web language and its additional features present more tracking opportunities because the technology uses a process in which large amounts of data can be collected and stored on the user's hard drive while online. Because of that process, advertisers and others could, experts say, see weeks or even months of personal data. That could include a user's location, time zone, photographs, text from blogs, shopping cart contents, e-mails and a history of the Web pages visited.[5]

This is what happened when I was searching for the baby presents and then received ads targeted to me from other baby apparel sites that I had not even visited. Web-based mail sites such as Google and Yahoo can also collect information on you. Search engines, Web mail, and social media all build profiles on you based on the things that you search for in a search box to target ads to you on that page or keywords from your mail. For example, if you are on a message board or using your Web mail and talking about cars, the Web mail or search engine site can pull keywords and, based on the text, target car ads directly to you in real time on that page. Such sites can also search for keywords in your mail and collect the data to piece together a profile on you to sell things to you or to other advertisers. By collecting and parsing your content and applying predictive analytics, they can personally tailor search results based on learning your life patterns. If you Google the word "puppies," chances are Google will give you back results that are local to your area, or in some other way tailored to your search or mail behavior. You can easily test this yourself. Go to a search engine and search for a particular topic. Ask a friend in another location to search using the same search engine for the same topic and compare your results. You might be surprised at how different and personally targeted the results are.

The Art of the Possible: Just How Good Are They at Getting Your Data?

Back in the early days of peer-to-peer networks (P2P), some people using P2P who wanted to share information from their hard drives failed to use the proper access controls on the software and allowed their entire hard drives to be shared with anyone who was using the same P2P program. This is still going on. Programs and apps could potentially have access to other programs or apps on your system. For example, if you don't like the standard SMS interface on your smartphone and choose to use another application to view and send your SMS messages, for the program to work, you have to give that secondary SMS app access to your SMS program, message history, and contact list. The makers of that secondary app could potentially collect your messages, history, contact list, and other items associated with SMS. Combined with your GEO coordinates and other information gleaned from your device, that secondary company could glean a lot of information about you. Most apps will tell you what they collect and do with your data in their terms of service, but they are not necessarily obligated to do so, especially if the company developing that app is in a country outside of the United States. This company might also have the ability to sell your data.

Applications are not necessarily stand-alone or self-contained. Other applications, depending on what access they have to your device, could potentially read and collect from other applications. A browser could potentially (like the misconfigured P2P mentioned previously) have access to other areas of your hard drive or device to collect information from other services or apps. For example, if you have sensitive documents open on your computer and you have your browser open, too, it is technically possible for the browser to read those documents. I am by no means stating that social media apps or browsers currently do collect or bleed into other areas, but it is feasible and not technically difficult to do, depending on what access they have other areas of the device. I was using a social media app on my smartphone and got an SMS message from a friend of mine that she also sent to three other people whom I had never met and did not have in my contact list. I began a private conversation with one of the other people on the SMS due to some similar interests. At the end of the private conversation, I added the person and her phone number to my contact list. After I went back to the social media app, the name of the woman I had just added to my phone's contact list, and whom I had never met or spoken with before, was suggested to me by the social media app as someone I might know and want to friend. This could have been a coincidence, and I am not saying it wasn't; however, it was a pretty strange coincidence! Moreover, because I know that it is technically possible and easy for the social media app to collect information from my SMS app and device, and then use it to suggest a connection, I immediately thought that this is what happened.

Let's see what a bad guy can do

Even if someone is targeting you and not using predicative analysis software, an ISP, or company whose app or site you are using, it can be surprisingly easy for an average person to put together a profile of another person based on online identities.

Let's say that I posted a photo to a Website such as 4chan.com from an account that was linked to me. You could download it (using a free tool typically found in forensic circles, called IrfanView[6]) and very easily view the EXIF data from the photo, including my GEO coordinates, which would look something like this:

DateTime: 2013:04:15 14:19:15
GPS information:
GPSLatitude: 38 51.75 0 (38.861833)
GPSLongitude: 77 22.49 0 (77.374500)

There is more information to be found in EXIF data, but I wanted to show you the information most relevant to what we're discussing here. Using the same program, I can plug in the GEO coordinates (I have slightly changed them) to Google Earth and see exactly where I was when I took that photo.

By simply following someone's location data and other content gleaned from social media, and by following the trail that the EXIF data in photos leaves for us, we can begin to piece together a person's habits. By using Google Earth, anyone can get a very good visual representation of where you have been and establish a pattern of your typical daily life. For example, if you were to follow me on social media that doesn't strip out EXIF data where I post photos, you could ascertain a lot of information about me. You could determine where I like to go and from where most of my posts originate, which you would assume is probably my home address. If you are using a social media site that strips out EXIF data from posted photos, maybe I post with my location services turned on. It would show the date and time and exactly where I was when I posted my update. Maybe I frequently talk about specific places that I go to, as most people do. For example, I might post, "Well, it's Friday, so we are off to Bollywood Bistro. Every time I go, I almost die over how good the food is." Anyone can use a search engine and see the exact location of Bollywood Bistro and ascertain, based on my words, that we probably go there every Friday.

Based on watching my location data and content from posts, you could probably ascertain and forecast the top 10 places where I spend my time, including where I work and where I will be on a typical Saturday at 10 a.m. Let's pretend that you are a bad guy and intend to do me harm. Simply by following my location postings and EXIF data, you could have determined that I moved from Arlington to Fairfax on March 16 because that was when suddenly all of my posting locations began to change from Arlington locations to those in Fairfax. Because of the location and EXIF data, you now have my address. You can also reverse-engineer and follow my former posts, and again assume that I am most often posting from my old home address. Now you have that, too. You see that I have dog named Horatio and no children. Even if I don't put my birthday in my social media profiles, you would notice when people tell me happy birthday. I post about my husband and the things that we like to do. By following my posts, you also can discover his birthday and our anniversary. You can glean who my friends and family are, and by following members of my family, you could find out things like my mother's maiden name and where I went to school. You would see when I got my new car because I posted a photo of it. In the photo, not only do you have the make and model of my car, but perhaps I accidently posted a picture of the car with the license plate. Now let's go to LinkedIn. You now have access to my current and all of my former employers. You can see endorsements from current and former work colleagues. You also see can see where my husband works. Now we can go online and do a search for even more personal information. You can easily get my phone number by paying a small fee. You can get access to any criminal charges, and you can see if I own a house where it is and how much I paid for it and how much it is worth. Sometimes you can get social security numbers from various court records, particularly divorce or bankruptcy records; some states post traffic violations online with social security numbers. Based on my posts, even if it is just a "like" for someone else's post, you can get a good idea of my politics, my interests, my personality—who I am as a person. Aside from the public records, most of this can be gleaned by things that I have chosen to self-disclose.

None of this information by itself is a big deal. But now, let's start to put together the puzzle pieces one by one. You have the following: my home address, my former address, my birthday, my husband's name and birthday, my dog's name (since I have no children, his name could be a password), the names of all my family members and their birthdays (maybe you get lucky and get my mother's maiden name), where I went to school, the make and model of my car and the date I bought it (you might even have the license plate), all of my work history including dates that I worked at each company (and you can probably ascertain who my supervisors were at each job), my husband's employment history, and my phone number. You may have even been lucky and gotten my social security number. This is a lot of information that, when put together, creates a very detailed picture of my life and person. This is not intended to scare you but to make you aware that the things you post yield a lot of information about you— more than you'd think—and to make you think a little bit harder about what you post and how it could be used against you.

What Can You Do to Protect Yourself?

This book is not intended to be a security guide. There are many excellent and useful guides on the Internet that can tell you how to secure and lock down your digital devices. However, we will discuss some of the basics. The most important thing is to become aware of what you look like online. Perform searches of yourself and begin to look through the things that you post in a timeline, just as someone who was trying to gather information about you would. It is almost impossible to fully remove information from the Internet. Once it is out there, it is out there. We go into greater detail on how content is never really gone and discuss cleaning services such as Reputation.com in a later chapter.

Rules to live and post by

Before posting anything, abide by the following rules:

1. You are not protected by privacy settings. Assume that everything that you post is viewable by everyone and anyone.

2. Anything that you post is posted forever and cannot be removed from the Internet. Even if you remove something, it is still "out there" somewhere.

3. If you wouldn't show it to everyone at a party, don't post it.

4. If you wouldn't walk up to your boss and say it or show it to her, don't post it.

5. If you're posting something that will hurt someone or is it is something that you wouldn't say to a person's face, don't post it.

6. If it is something that will someday haunt, embarrass, or hurt your children, don't post it.

7. If you are very angry, wait a day before posting. Posting something in this state almost always ends up in regret by the poster.

8. Like "drunk dialing," never post while intoxicated.

Knowledge is power: read and understand the terms of service (TOS)

Understand that knowledge is power. Before you sign up for any service, Website, or app, carefully read the terms of service and familiarize yourself with the privacy options and settings. Most terms of service will tell you exactly what information they collect about you and how they use your content, usually in pretty easy-to-understand language.

Private browsing

Most browsers have the "private browser" or "incognito" function, which will not save regular cookies to your device. Each time you navigate to a favorite site using this feature, it is like starting a brand-new session, as if you had never been to that site before. The private browsing function will accept the cookie from a Website and then delete it when you close the session. Firefox and Chrome can enable private or incognito browsing for Android devices. Chrome has an app that allows incognito browsing for IOS so will work on most iPhones and iPads. It is important to understand that this does not make you anonymous; ISPs and sites can still track you.

Private browsing will not save:

- **Visited pages:** No pages will be added to the list of sites in the History menu, the Library window's history list, or the Awesome Bar address list.

- **Form and Search Bar entries:** Nothing you enter into text boxes on web pages or the Search bar will be saved for Form autocomplete.

- **Passwords:** No new passwords will be saved.

- **Download List entries:** No files you download will be listed in the Downloads Window after you turn off Private Browsing.

- **Cookies:** Cookies store information about websites you visit such as site preferences, login status, and data used by plugins like Adobe Flash. Cookies can also be used by third parties to track you across websites. For more info about tracking, see How do I turn on the Do-not-track feature?

- **Cached Web Content** and **Offline Web Content and User Data:** No temporary Internet files (cached files) or files that Websites save for offline use will be saved.[7]

Delete cookies, history, and cache

If you do not want to use private browsing but still do not want remnants of your activities on your computer, make sure that you regularly clear your browsing history and cache and delete your cookies. It is important to understand that by deleting these items from your hard drive or other device, you are only preventing *your* access to them. Also of note: Reformatting does not necessarily remove data. In most cases, forensic tools can very easily bring back the "deleted" items because the file is still there until it is overwritten. When you delete a file from most operating systems, you are technically only removing the link to be able to access the file. The only way to really remove the file from your device is to "wipe" it using a cleaning program such as the free program CCleaner[8], which zeros over the space multiple times where the file resided. Even then there are tools that can potentially bring back the item(s).

Turn off EXIF data and choose location services wisely

Without EXIF data in photographs, social media sites and applications cannot pull your location data out of your photographs. Also, people downloading your photos from social media sites that keep EXIF data in the photos will not be able to ascertain information about you from your EXIF data. You have the option of turning off location service on your device. For Android and Apple IOS, you would go into the Settings and turn off EXIF data for photographs. Also. think about allowing applications to access your location data when asked.

Also, to be able to use the applications and services that we have come to rely on, we have to provide at least *some* information about ourselves. Yes, there are a few things you can do to manage your privacy, but remember that knowledge is power. It is very easy for anyone to piece together a pattern of life on each based on what you post. But don't lose heart: As we will discuss in the following chapters, you have the ability to control your online image and make it appear exactly as you want it to appear.

\> <(((((o\>

Perception Is Everything

In the 1980s a popular advertisement for Head and Shoulders shampoo touted that "you never get a second chance to make a first impression." This statement could not be more true. Additionally, if you make a positive first impression, you will have an easy time living up that impression. If you make a negative first impression, however, you will have a very difficult time changing others' perceptions of you. That is why making the first impression a good one is so important. Making a good first impression can be the deciding factor in whether or not you will get the job or the date, or whether you'll have a good personal or professional relationship with someone. Most of us are not aware of the first impression we make on others; it just isn't something that we think about.

We meet new people every day and we are constantly assessing and appraising them, whether we realize it or not.

Others are also assessing us. In order to make this process of assessment easier, our brains collect and store memories and learned associations in a kind of personal database. Learned associations can include assumptions such as "sloppy dress equals laziness." Or we might associate good posture with confidence, or fidgeting with shiftiness and untrustworthiness, or a cold, clammy handshake with an unsavory character. We may dislike someone simply because we associate her perfume with someone we had a falling out with years ago. When we meet someone new, we access this database to determine whether we are encountering a friend or foe, and whether we have common ground with this person. We are constantly subconsciously judging others based on this personal database of memories and associations, and the whole process happens in only a fraction of a second. A study done in 2009 by Princeton University psychologist Alex Todorov determined that people make this initial assessment in just one-tenth of a second.[1] One-tenth of a second is an incredibly short amount of time to come up with a clear and lasting first impression! It may seems unbelievable that we can decide whether or not we like or trust someone so quickly, but we can and we do. And it all happens without our conscious knowledge.

Most of us want to create the impression that we are confident, trustworthy, kind, attractive, hardworking, decent, and likeable. So how do we do this in a mere one-tenth of a second? There are a lot of great books on the market that teach readers rules on how to understand and use facial expressions and body language to project a desired impression. These rules are great for making a good first impression and maintaining your image in the physical world, but what about in the virtual world, where we don't have the luxury of using and reading body language? How can we make a good first impression online? Well, it really isn't that different. It is important to understand that people are still accessing and using their inner databases when judging your online persona. People will still assess you almost instantly and then create a perception of you simply based on your activities online. This chapter will show how you may be unknowingly misrepresenting yourself online, and what you can do to fix that. I will also discuss how people perceive and define your personality based on how and what you post.

At this point, most of us know and expect that potential employers will investigate our online activities before hiring us; or, if we are currently employed, they may periodically check up on us. Many companies have image and morality clauses in their employment contracts and they want to make sure that you are adhering to those contractual requirements. Remember, even though you have your personal life, you still represent your employer even when you're not at work. Therefore, it's important when you are posting to social media or other sites that you try to see your posts as a stranger or potential employer might. You need to make sure that you are not being perceived and labeled, however inadvertently, as someone you are not. When you walk into a room with bad posture or make aggressive gestures such as pointing or eye-rolling, you can be perceived and labeled, variously, as lazy, unsure, or cocky. This kind of mislabeling can happen online, too, simply based on your posting habits, what you post, and your posting personality. What potential employers and colleagues think of you, however misguided or inaccurate, will undoubtedly impact your hiring and promotion potential, raises, projects that you may be assigned, and your overall career trajectory. Pretty powerful stuff!

What You Might Be Doing Wrong

Remember, you want to project an image of yourself as someone who is confident, professional, and, above all, age appropriate. Look at the postings in the following example and try to determine the age of Jane Doe:

> **Jane Doe:** OMG...Such fun with the girls last night... too bad all the boys were total WEAK SAUCE
>
> **Jane Doe:** So Totes excited to see Jenny my BFF tonight.
>
> **Jane Doe:** Boss = totes weak sauce; new project = even more totes weak sauce
>
> **Jane Doe:** New boy at office...Major hottie..def not not not weak sauce

Would you be surprised to find out that the posts came from a professional woman in her 50s? If her boss, colleagues, potential employers, or experts in her vocational community saw these posts, they would most likely think of her in the same way they would if she always wore clothing that was too young for her age. In short, she would not be taken seriously.

The single post vs. the whole identity

Along with posting using age-appropriate and proper professional terminology, there are certain posting habits that you want to avoid. People will judge you on *all* of your posted content. When you post content, you are most likely thinking in the moment about that particular single post, but when someone else is looking at your online persona *in toto*, they will be looking at the whole picture and putting all of your posts together to define who you are. This is why you need to think about every single post you make as being part of a larger picture. Look at the following post and think about the impression it yields of the poster:

March 1, 2013

> **Jane Doe:** I am really tired and wanted to go to sleep an hour ago but devil baby won't go to sleep again.

This post is innocuous by itself. Jane is tired, and we can all feel for her, having a small child who is keeping her from getting sleep. We might feel sympathetic toward Jane and perceive her as doing the best she can. Calling her child "devil baby" might seem funny in this context. But watch the pattern emerge when you put multiple posts together:

March 1, 2013

> **Jane Doe:** I am really tired and wanted to go to sleep an hour ago but devil baby won't go to sleep again

March 2, 2013

> **Jane Doe:** So tired. Four days with no lunch break. I work with idiots and devil baby kept me up again all night.

March 2, 2013

> **Jane Doe:** OMG so stressed out. I hate my job. Just need sleep. Why won't this devil child sleep?

March 2, 2013

> **Jane Doe:** Well Husband stayed late at work again meaning that I have to make dinner and get the kids ready for bed all by myself again. Devil Baby is super cranky. Sometimes I can't stand this kid. Probably won't get any sleep again tonight.

March 3, 2013

> **Jane Doe:** I have today off. Yay! Between Baby and the idiots at work, I didn't sleep worth crap last night.

March 3, 2013

> **Jane Doe:** What a crappy day off. Husband worked late again and of course did nothing around the house to help out. So bad that I am breaking the diet.

March 3, 2013

> **Jane Doe:** Why does this kid cry so much? Go the f$*k to sleep.

When you put these posts together, a totally different picture of this person emerges. She seems fed up and stressed out but also comes across as not able to handle the pressure of being a working mother. Most likely, she is just venting and does not mean to come across as a constant complainer; however, when you have nothing else to judge her by except for these posts, she comes across as extremely negative and even a bit unbalanced. She posts nothing but complaints about her work and her baby. She thinks of her colleagues as idiots, which might make some think of her as arrogant. She refers to her child multiple times as "devil baby," which is going to be hurtful to that child someday when he/she is old enough to read the posts. Overall, the impression that you get of her is that she is not a happy person. When I showed these posts to various people, the reaction I got was almost always the same: The perception was that she seems disrespectful and arrogant, and looks down on her peers, colleagues, boss, and husband. If you were making a hiring decision based on these posts, there is a good chance that you would not want to employ her.

Again, when we are posting, we tend to think in the moment instead of remaining cognizant about how all the puzzle pieces fit together. I can't stress how important it is in creating your online identity and controlling the perceptions of others that you look at each post in terms of how it fits into the big picture and not just as a single post, because that is how others will see it.

How We Are Actually Perceived vs. How We *Think We Are Being Perceived*

Even though some social media sites will allow you to post content that only specifically defined "circles" of friends can access, we need to remember that social media rules on privacy can change. At some point, those closely controlled, private circles might be accessible to anyone. So even when you are posting to "private" circles, post content that maintains and supports the image that you want others to see. HR professionals now have the luxury of using social media to get to know a candidate. This is great for companies, because it costs a lot of money to hire, train, and retain employees. HR professionals can learn a lot about a potential candidate by viewing social media sites and using the techniques discussed in chapters 8 and 9. By employing these techniques, they can determine if someone is being truthful on his or her resume.

HR professionals can and do use body language techniques during an interview to vet potential candidates. However, as we learned in Chapter 2, the bevy of information gleaned from someone's online profile is a much better way to gauge who a person really is and what makes him or her tick. You could be an expert in your field, but if you can't get along with a team or don't take direction well, you could be considered a risky choice. This is important to keep in the back of your mind each and every time you post.

Posting Styles

There are a few posting styles that are much more likely to cause others to label you incorrectly, so you want to make sure that your posting style does not fall into any of these categories. Of course, we all occasionally lapse and post something that could fall into one of these categories, but what you want to avoid is *always* posting in one or more of these ways. For this section, I showed a diverse group of people, including HR professionals and hiring managers, the following examples and asked them how they perceived the poster. I have added the most common labels and keywords used to describe each personality type.

The one-upper

Examples:

Poster: My son David just started walking at one year old!

One-Upper: That's great! My son Sage was walking at 6 months...however, he is much smarter than most children his age.

Poster: I just finished the so-and-so marathon.

One-Upper: Oh yeah, I did that marathon too and five others, but you should still be proud of yourself.

This is the person who will always post something that "one-ups" what others post. The group surveyed most commonly described this person as arrogant and annoying. All of the HR professionals said that if they read a profile that consistently showed this posting style, they would not hire this person because they would be concerned that he or she wouldn't work well with a team and wouldn't be able to accept direction from authority figures. This is extremely important to think about when you are posting. Let's say that someone is discussing a topic that you are experienced with or an expert in. You can share your knowledge, but you must do it in such a way that does not make you appear to be one-upping the other person. There are exceptions, however: In some professions, this type of posting style can be seen as advantageous. For example, if you were an HR person at a law firm looking to hire someone with good arguing skills, you might look for someone who exhibited the traits of a one-upper.

The over-sharer

Examples:

Over-Sharer: I went to the store

Over-Sharer: I bought chicken for dinner

Over-Sharer: Boy that chicken was awesome

Over-Sharer: I am watching TV

Over-Sharer: Boy this show is good

Over-Sharer: Time to use the restroom

These are the people who tell the world all about the excruciating minutiae of their lives. Most members of the polled group stated that they thought that this person just felt the need to share, but that he or she came off as self-important, entitled, or bored and directionless. Again, it is important to note that the HR professionals in the group said that they would be concerned about hiring this person. They felt that this person would likely get too bogged down by details and would have a hard time completing tasks on time. A few even said that they would be concerned that this person would be too busy posting to social media to get his or her work done.

The boundary-crosser

Examples:

Boundary-Crosser: Well my ex just dropped off the kids. She fed them McDonalds again which means that I now have to be the bad guy once again by feeding them healthy food for the next few days.

Boundary-Crosser: Well looks as if I now have to fix my boss's stupid mistake...AGAIN! He actually had the nerve to complain that I came to work late today and didn't finish my report on time.

The polled group felt as if this person was posting this way because he was angry and vindictive about something, and wanted to punish others by airing his dirty laundry. The HR professionals said that they would not hire him because he came across as unprofessional, immature, and downright mean. There was also the fear that this person might not be able to keep company trade secrets confidential. It is one thing to discuss your dirty laundry with close friends or family, but quite another to fight your battles online for everyone to see.

The arguer

Examples:

Poster: I read that stripes are the new spring fashion trend

Arguer: That is so last year. The current spring trend is lime green.

Poster: Oh well, *X Fashion Magazine* said that stripes were in

Arguer: *X Fashion Magazine* does not and never has accurately forecasted the trends right. The newest trend is lime green, according to source 1, source 2, source 3....

This person will passionately argue about anything and everything in order to prove that she is right, no matter what. The polled group felt that this person probably just felt very passionate about the topic (spring trends), but that she still came off as arrogant, uncompromising, and unable to work well with others. Of all of the personality types, this is the one that the HR professionals felt the most strongly about. They viewed this person as unable to work in a team and unable to understand and work within a chain of command.

The Eeyore

Examples:

Eeyore: I got no sleep again. The kids kept me up all night

Eeyore: God my day was so hard. I really need a drink

Eeyore: The boss just dumped a ton more work on me when I already have too much to do

Eeyore: Kids are sick again. I guess I have to take off work again and go to the doctor. Probably means that I will get sick too

This person is probably just depressed and overwhelmed and wants a sympathetic ear. However, he is generally perceived as a complainer, someone who is unable to handle the day-to-day challenges we all face. The HR professionals I polled said that they would have to think long and hard about hiring this person. They felt as if he would be difficult to work with, would probably make excuses as to why he couldn't meet deadlines, and would most likely miss a lot of work.

The sexy picture girl

This person is probably looking for validation and is most likely insecure. The survey group perceived this person as sad, desperate, and seeking attention. She was also perceived as immature and unprofessional.

The party-time player

This person will often refer to himself using words like "pimpin'" and "sexy," and is always posting photos of himself partying. This posting style comes across as extremely unprofessional (and can actually get you fired, depending on your company's expectations of conduct).

Example:

Party-time: [with photo of himself shirtless, drinking shots] Check out this hot body!! Pimpin' like a gangster with my peeps...

Interestingly, most of the people I polled were alarmed that they, too, had made the mistake of posting things like this. A few of them immediately checked their social media posts! It is important to remember that everyone occasionally posts content that falls into one of these categories, but the key is to not *always* post that type of content and to become more aware of how you could come across, based on your posts.

Managing Your Image Online

So now that you know that people will judge you based on all of your content and not just individual posts, and now that you understand what posting styles can lead to negative perceptions, let's look at ways to begin the process of controlling your image. Becoming aware of your posting style and content is the first step to managing your online identity. The next thing that we have to do is look through all of your content as though it were created by someone else. You need to look with an unbiased eye and pretend as if you were reading someone else's content, making an impression of who this person is, and figuring out what makes him or her tick.

Answer the following questions about your content as if you were an HR professional:

- What impression do you have of this person?

- Does this person's style fit into one of the previous categories?

- If so, which one? How often?

- Would people want to be friends or work with this person?

- How could this person change the way he or she posts to improve his or her image?

- What makes this person unique and special, and what do you like the most about him or her?

Framing and reframing

Now that you've answered these questions, we're ready to talk about how to frame your posts so that they appear the way you want them to appear. First I must preface this by saying that I am by no means advocating lying or trying to be someone you are not. Nor do I want you to become so self-conscious about posting that you become a boring, "Stepford" version of who you really are. That is why answering the last question is especially important. This is not about pretending that everything is perfect all of the time, because people will (correctly) perceive that as phoniness. We are simply going to tweak the content that you feel doesn't show you in the best light, in order to frame it differently. Simply by reframing your posts, you can create a completely different image and hence control the perceptions of others.

Framing is a way of presenting something—a person, a situation, an event—differently. In law enforcement, it is a calculated technique used to get someone to talk to you and/or want to help you. For example, a police officer friend of mine told me that when he wanted to find out if a suspect had prior arrests, he would use the framing technique to structure his question in a certain way. Instead of asking, "Have you been arrested before?" which would most likely yield a deceitful answer, he would ask, "What was last thing you were arrested for?" When the question was framed this way—in a way that indicated that my officer friend actually already knew the answer—the suspect would typically be more truthful. You can use framing in a similar manner when you post your content. If Jane Doe from the first example were to simply reframe her situation, we would see her in a completely different light. So instead of saying, "I am really tired and wanted to go to sleep an hour ago but devil baby won't go to sleep again," let's reframe the content as follows: "Being a new mother is really hard. I am really tired and wanted to go to sleep an hour ago but I can't get the baby to sleep. Any suggestions?" Everyone who was shown this revised post felt that this is a tired new mother who is acknowledging that she needs help. She is taking the initiative and looking for solutions to her problems by asking fellow new mothers what has worked for them. This makes her look like a self-starter. She knows she has a problem, but instead of just complaining and being defeatist, she is inviting suggestions, which makes her look like a team player. Moreover, she is tech-savvy enough to use crowdsourcing to help solve her problem. The perception we have of her is now very different, isn't it?

You might not master framing overnight, but if you continue to work at it and really answer the questions honestly, you will eventually get the hang of it. We will discuss many more similar helpful tips to manage your online persona in Chapter 5.

Friends of a Feather, Flock Together

One final concept that I would like to discuss in this chapter is the idea that "friends of a feather, flock together." In high school, you were probably defined by the clique or cliques you hung out with. The geeks, the jocks, the popular girls and guys—they all hung out together. Members of each clique dressed the same and even spoke the same, so it was easy to determine what clique someone belonged to simply based on how that person looked. There was probably also a general perception of what the people in each clique were like—for example, maybe the popular girls were viewed as mean, or the jocks were perceived as dumb. Most people know that perceptions will not apply to every member of a group. You could have a very sweet, kind popular girl, a valedictorian jock, or a not-too-bright geek. However, because each clique had a predetermined reputation, you were defined and stereotyped by outsiders based on your clique's reputation, unless someone outside of that group got to know you personally.

Even if we are 10, 15, 20 years out of high school, we tend to lump people together into groups or cliques, even in the work world, and then we slap labels on them. Whether or not this is fair, you are defined by the company you keep in the real world—and online. It is relatively easy for someone to determine who your closest friends are based on who tags you or whom you tag in photographs, as well as based on the content you post. For example, someone who merely likes my posted content but never appears in photos or rarely engages with me is probably not a close friend. But someone whose bridal shower I attend and post photos of or have much more intimate conversation with could be seen as a closer friend. The lesson here is that it is a good idea to take stock of your social media friends. You want to make sure that the people you are associated with don't paint negative pictures of themselves because you could be lumped into the same category. Not only do companies and organizations judge you based on your friends, but a new trend is evolving wherein companies are now making important financial decisions about you based on your social media friends. If you don't believe me, just read this:

Facebook friends could change your credit score

A handful of tech startups are using social data to determine the risk of lending to people who have a difficult time accessing credit. Traditional lenders rely heavily on credit scores like FICO, which look at payments history. They typically steer clear of the millions of people who don't have credit scores. But some financial lending companies have found that social connections can be a good indicator of a person's creditworthiness. Using "big data" to assess credit risk is on the verge of going mainstream.[2]

This is a scary but potentially real concept. You could be negatively affecting your future ability to secure a mortgage, get good interest rates, or acquire credit simply because of the company you keep online. This is not meant to scare you, but to make you more aware of whom you choose to associate with on social media. Fair or not, moral or not, you *will* be judged and defined by others based on your posted content. This is not all gloom and doom, though: By raising your awareness and making just a few tweaks to how you post, you now have the power to control the image you put out there and, therefore, how others will perceive you.

4

Smarter Social:
Building Rapport Online

<*(((>< <0))))x

With the advent of social media, everyone now has the potential to be a public figure. I often hear people comparing how many social media followers they have, defining their self-worth based on that number, which is ridiculous. Unless you are a blogger by trade, a public figure, or someone who uses social media as part of your work (a marketing manager, for example), quality is more important than quantity; it is more important to have the *right* social media contacts as friends and connections. You want to have friends who can help you get what you want, rather than arbitrarily friending anyone you come into contact with, just to pad your numbers. This book will not teach you how to be a major influencer, how to amass millions of followers, or how to go viral. The point is to teach you how to manage your image to get the things you want, personally and professionally, and to protect yourself and your children while doing so.

The Importance of Building Rapport

In the real world, to get people on your side, and effectively influence the situation and elicit the responses you seek, you must build rapport with them, whether it is a boss, colleague, professional expert, or friend. Building rapport means finding common ground with someone, getting that person to connect with you and essentially view you as a friend or trusted confidant. Building rapport and effectively building successful relationships applies in business settings, with friends, and in negotiations in daily life. Studies show that people tend to gravitate toward people who are similar to them. We are most comfortable with people who are familiar to us and who share our interests, values, style of dress, and so on.

Think about your friends or the work colleagues you like spend time with. In most cases, you will find that you like them because you have something in common with them, even if it is something as simple as a love for a particular sport, TV show, or activity. We tend to feel uncomfortable with people who are different from us. So how can you use building rapport to your advantage? The first step to building rapport with a person is to do a little research and familiarize yourself with your target of interest. This can be traditional, primary research, or on-the-spot research. This is important whether you will be presenting to an audience, attending a meeting at work, going on a job interview, meeting strangers at a party, connecting with a potential client, or vetting your child's new teacher. If you have time, find out something about the person or group. Speak to someone who knows the person or has spoken to that audience before. Find out what worked for him or her and what didn't. Find out if there is a particular topic or interest that your target has; they might be huge sports fans, for example, and you might be, too. You can use that common ground as a rapport builder. We will discuss in detail how to use the Internet to research people online in the Recon section of this chapter. For now, just know that the key to building rapport with people, whether in the real world or online, is finding something that gets them talking. Knowing beforehand what someone's interests are will help you to ask the right questions and use rapport to build a successful relationship.

I learned about building successful rapport with an audience the hard way. Prior to working in the federal Intelligence Community (IC), I worked supporting federal, state, and local law enforcement (LE), which was a very different and open community. In the LE world, people freely speak with each other in professional environments. Trust is much more easily given, and collaboration is a rule rather than an exception. When I worked in LE, I gave presentations at LE conferences frequently, all over the country. I briefed many various LE groups and taught computer forensic examination courses. During these presentations, I used techniques that would get the audience involved and participating in an interactive way, which was always met with success. I prided myself on being able to build rapport with the audience. The enthusiasm was always present in the audience, and I felt great about my ability to successfully get my points across. Often LE participants would line up after the presentations to ask more questions. LE audiences were incredibly easy to engage. They even laughed at my very stupid jokes. I began to consider myself a pretty good speaker and loved doing it.

My first presentation that I had to give in the IC was to an audience of very seasoned Special Forces operatives. It was during my first few weeks on the job. I was a little nervous, but I calmed my nerves by telling myself that I had done this countless times and that I was an engaging speaker who knew how to build rapport with an audience. My boss warned me that this crowd might be different from what I was used to. He told me that it would take a long time for them to trust me enough to open up to me, and that I might not get a welcome reception until they got to know me better. I shrugged off his advice, thinking that I would have no problem as long as I started off with a joke. That had always worked before. I would have this crowd eating out of my hand in no time—or so I thought.

I approached the podium and began my presentation by opening with a joke that I'd used many times prior: "Don't worry, we only have 500 PowerPoint slides to get through!" Not a single laugh. Not even a smile. No gestures or movement from the audience. There were 20 pairs of eyes staring at me, sizing me up. I knew right away that I was in trouble. I asked the audience a question to lighten things up, but again I felt 20 pairs of eyes staring at me and got no answer. Somehow I made it through, but you can imagine how my confidence in my presentation style took a serious nose dive. Not a single person came up to me after the presentation or introduced him- or herself. I knew then that my previous LE style of speaking would not work in this community; I had to adapt quickly and do some research to learn how to build rapport with the IC audience. Now, years later, I am very close to this particular group and have briefed them successfully many times. But I had to completely change my presentation style to fit this new audience. That day, I learned a very important lesson (the hard way) about building rapport with a person or an audience: *You have to know your audience.* What may work with some people may not work with others. If you don't have the time to research your audience, you will have to learn to adapt your style quickly by gauging your audience on the fly—difficult, but not impossible.

Conducting Recon on a Target

So now that we understand how crucial building rapport with an audience or another person is to our success, we have to learn how to do a little reconnaissance using whatever tools we have, including the Internet and social media. To build rapport with someone you don't know, you'll probably need to do a little research. Remember, people like people who are similar to them or with whom they have some common ground. As you learned in Chapter 2, there is a lot of free information available online that you can use to build rapport with your target.

Time capsules

Websites such as the Wayback Machine at Archive.org "crawl" open Internet sites, collecting data and keeping records of how Websites look at a particular date and time. Let's say that you have an interview with an engineering company called Smith and Sons. Obviously you'll want to do some research on the company so that you don't go in blind. So you visit the company Website and see that a woman named Dana Smith is the current CEO. Now that you have a name, you can do some research on her. On the Website, you can navigate through and familiarize yourself with the services that the company provides. This will help you appear knowledgeable about the company during the interview. But what if you want to take it a step further and show that you stand apart from other potential candidates? What if you want more extensive knowledge of the company, including its past history? Using the Wayback Machine on Archive.org, you do a little digging and see that the previous CEO was named John Doe, and that the current CEO took the helm in 2010. There are also extensive bios about both Mr. Doe and Ms. Smith. You also discover that in 2008, the company provided 14 services, but now boasts 23 services. Imagine how much more impressive your interview will be if you know these facts, facts that the average candidate won't know. It will show the hiring manager that you are interested and have invested time getting to know the company. If you use your facts wisely, you will stand out from the pack. You've successfully done recon on your target (in this case, a company).

Social media

When conducting recon on a specific person, you may or may not want that person to know that you've been looking her up. At the time of this writing, if you view a target's profile using Facebook, there is no way for that target to know that you looked at her profile. This is true even if you view her profile while logged in to your own Facebook page. That said, keep in mind that Facebook will have a record of the time and date that you viewed your target and will maintain that record, just as it states it will in its terms of service (TOS).

LinkedIn is a different story. If you are logged in with your LinkedIn credentials, your target will know that you viewed his profile; it will even offer the target a link to your profile.

If you want to browse anonymously on LinkedIn, there are a few things that you can do to remain hidden. First, you can make sure that you are not logged in to LinkedIn with your credentials while viewing your target's profile. Instead, use a search engine and link to his page from there. (Make sure that you haven't been "auto logged in" by deleting all cookies associated with LinkedIn.) Another option is to set your privacy settings in your LinkedIn profile such that when you view a profile, you will show up to your target as an anonymous member. This way, the target will know that *someone* looked at his profile, but he won't know who.

Sometimes you'll actually want a target to know that you were looking at his profile. This can get your target interested in who you are, and make him want to seek you out and look at your profile, in turn. For example, if you are interviewing for a job and you know the hiring manager's name, you might want the hiring manager to know that you looked her up. This shows the hiring manager that you did your due diligence. She will probably be curious enough to look at your profile, which will help keep you fresh in her mind. With today's job market as tight as it is, anything you can do to stand out or be memorable in a hiring manager's mind will increase your chances of getting the job.

Because we know that people tend to be more personal on Facebook than they are on professional social media sites such as LinkedIn, you might want to conduct recon on a target's Facebook page. Most people apply some sort of privacy settings to their Facebook profile and do not allow just anyone to view all the content on their pages. Typically, most Facebook users will adjust their privacy settings so that friends of friends can view their profiles. Even if your target has her privacy settings pretty locked down, at the time of this writing, you will still be able to see who her friends are. If you want to research a target but not necessarily send her a friend request, you can sometimes do your recon through one of your target's friends. Almost everyone has at least one Facebook friend who has no privacy settings, an open page, and/or many Facebook friends. Keep in mind that unless you are famous, most people do not have hundreds of close personal friends. It is likely that this person is a friend collector and will accept a friend request from a stranger. It is also highly likely that your target will be friends with at least one friend collector. Using your Facebook page and credentials, you can send a friend request to your target's collector friend. If your target allows friends of friends to view her page, you now have full access without ever having to friend her personally. If friending a friend doesn't work, another less savory technique you can use is the fake profile. I don't recommend this technique, however, especially because it is against Facebook's and LinkedIn's TOS. As well, if your target is adept at detecting deception, she will easily be able to determine that your profile is fake.

If you are doing recon and want to follow someone's Twitter feed, most are open to the public. If you only want to read his Twitter feed, your target won't know you're doing this. However, if you wish to follow your target, he *will* know that you are following him.

Search engines

Along with social media recon, don't discount old-fashioned search engines. Using search engines will give you access to public information such as arrest records, home ownership, driving records, and other useful pools of information. Google will also link you to any blogs (such a Tumblr) or blog postings created or owned by your target.

Photo search and compare

Photo searching has become very advanced. If you have a photo of your target, there are many easy-to-use and free photo-searching tools at your disposal, such as TinEye[1] or Google Image Search[2], to see if you can find photos of your target elsewhere on the Internet. Become familiar with these free photo-searching tools. If you have a photo of your target, use these photo-search tools to see if the same photos pop up anywhere else. Even if your target has a very small Internet presence or doesn't give away many personal details, through photo searching, you may be able to find an exact match for that photo on another Website—a site devoted to sailing, for example, where the target is using another name. This gives you a clue that your target has a hobby as a sailor, but also that he is going by another name on the Internet. Now you can conduct Google searches of the target using this secondary name. Perhaps under this second name he is active on secondary social media sites where he is giving away much more personal information.

Getting to Know You: Baselining

Once you have access to a target's social media sites and have done your due diligence using search engines, you can begin the process of building a pattern, or a baseline, of your target in order to determine just how to build rapport. Remember, you have a lot of information at your disposal, such as where your target went to school, where he works and lives, whether he has kids, who his best friends are, whether he has a pet, photographs of him (possibly with date/time stamps), his hobbies and interests, and where he spends his their time, based on his location data. But we can take it a step further. Based on his content, does your target have a sarcastic sense of humor? Does he seem to be agreeable, or does he fit into one of personality/posting types outlined in the previous chapter? You can begin to build a pattern of how this person talks based on the content of his posts and the banter he has with his friends. Even if someone is very careful not to discuss his political views, we can see if he happens to "like" a friend's political posting or an article about a political topic. In this way, you can really get to know your target in detail.

You can also use the public records you found using search engines to see if your target has been involved in a legal case or has an arrest record. You can also use public Websites to determine whether the target owns a house, how much he paid for it, and exactly where he lives.

Typically, even if posters don't use their e-mail addresses when posting to sensitive blogs, they will tend to use similar-sounding names. For example, I use my own name to post on Websites or blogs; but if I don't want someone to know who I am, I will use my dog's name. If you were to do a little research on my social media sites, you would be able to determine that I used to use this name frequently. You could then search for postings under that secondary name to see whether there were any juicy blog posts that would tell you more about me.

A lot of details can be gleaned from the friends that your target associates with. Perhaps even more can be determined by the friends that he *doesn't* have. For example, perhaps your target's LinkedIn page lists his work history; you see that he worked for company X from 2008 to 2010, for company Y from 2010 to 2011, and for company Z from 2011 to the present. If he has a bunch of connections from company X who have endorsed his skills, and many connections and endorsements from company Z, but no connections or endorsements from company Y, this should raise a red flag. Why doesn't he have friends or endorsements from company Y, the company he worked for from 2010 to 2011? What happened there? If you are an HR professional, it might be worth investigating. It may be nothing—perhaps company Y had only two employees and the other person moved to Antarctica where there is no Internet service. However, chances are good that there is something there that the target does not want others to know. An exception would be if your target has listed companies on his LinkedIn profile that existed before social media, such as in the 1990s or early 2000s, and he only has a few or no friends from those companies. In this case, you shouldn't necessarily be concerned. People lose touch and don't often search out people they worked with from 10 years ago or beyond.

I rarely use my Twitter account. However, I do post on occasion. I recently received an e-mail from Twitter stating that my account had potentially been compromised. I went to Twitter and saw that my account had indeed been compromised and that someone had posted something that I obviously (to me) would not have said. How did Twitter know this? Twitter had built a baseline of me and my habits. Twitter knew the unique, identifying details of the devices that I used to set up, maintain, and post content. It knew my operating systems, my IP addresses, my browser, my typical geocoordinates, and much other information that was and is unique to me. But it was also able to baseline my posting habits and style of speech, and determine that this particular post didn't come from me. Based on how I use words and grammar, the speed with which I type, and the kind of content I post, Twitter had a pretty good inkling that the post in question didn't come from me.

Twitter and other social media sites use sophisticated automated tools to piece together the unique pattern or signature of a person, but it is something that can be done manually, too. Everyone has a unique way of speaking, writing, and putting words together; everyone has a unique vocabulary. By learning a person's unique vocabulary and speech pattern, you can create signature that you know to be him. You are baselining him! Our individual patterns of speaking are subconscious. When we type or write, we tend to draw on the same subconscious pattern. Most people also have typical typing speed that can easily be used as a unique signature to determine who they are.

My husband, Matt, is very close with my brother Zayne, and often exchanges texts with him. Last year, Matt was trying to coordinate a trip with Zayne. We were coming from different sides of the country and meeting in Las Vegas. Zayne asked Matt what time our flight was getting in. Matt asked me to respond to my brother's text message because he was busy walking the dog.

I texted, "UA flght X gets in at 12. Cant wait to see you tmrw."

Zayne responded, "This is Tyler."

How did he know? From experience, he knew that I type very fast and that I typically abbreviate words, such as "flght" and "tmrw," when texting. He knew that Matt wouldn't have bothered to give him the airline and flight number and that I always do. He knew that Matt always uses proper punctuation and grammar and never abbreviates words in text messages. He had texted frequently enough with both of us to know our unique signatures of texting and to recognize that it was me. Without even realizing that he was doing it, Zayne had baselined both of our texting styles and was easily able tell the difference.

To help you build rapport with people, as well as for your own image management, you should be aware of your unique posting pattern and style so that you can tweak it if necessary. For example, if you are texting with a potential boss and she always uses punctuation, you will also want to use punctuation. It is important to note here that people can have very different baselines, or unique signatures, when using different media. For example, when I text or tweet, I use abbreviated words and don't always use punctuation. However, in e-mail or on LinkedIn, I always do. When using Facebook, I tend to be more lax.

Quick questions to ask to help baseline a target's style (will be different for different media):

- *How quickly does this person type?*

- *Does she use punctuation?*

- *Does she spell correctly?*

- *Does she use abbreviated words? If so, start to recognize the words she abbreviates.*

- *Are there any words that she seems to like to use? If so, what are they?*

- *How would you characterize her sense of humor?*

- *Does she type long and detailed sentences, or short, to-the-point, succinct ones?*

By answering the questions in the box, you can quickly baseline a unique, identifying signature for yourself, your friends, and your colleagues.

Companies also use this baselining technique for marketing. Researchers from the University of Cambridge determined that based on Facebook "likes" alone, highly personal attributes such as age, race, addictive behavior, political views, personality traits, gender, intelligence, and sexual orientation could be determined with great accuracy.[3] Certain quantitative behaviors determine real-world characteristics, and these behaviors can be applied to vetting an online persona. So why is this important? Remember that when building rapport with others, you want to appear like them. You want to use similar words and style of speech when reaching out and communicating. The more you know about a person, the better your chances will be of building successful rapport and getting what you want, in your personal and professional relationships.

Making Contact With Your Target

Now that you have learned how to baseline and conduct reconnaissance, you are ready to reach out to your target, whether it is in the form of an interview, a client meeting, or a speaking engagement. The first thing to remember is that you must be careful with the information that you have gleaned from your recon and baselining, because you don't want to come across as *too* knowledgeable.

An HR professional friend of mine, I'll call her Chris, works for a major government contractor. I asked her if any of the many interviews she had conducted were particularly memorable. She said that two in particular stood out. In one, she asked the candidate what he had done to prepare for the interview. He said he had used the Internet to research the company, the department, HR, and hiring managers that he'd be working for. The candidate said that based on the research, he felt as if his experience would fit in nicely and listed the reasons why. He knew that the company had just lost a major contract, and because he had experience writing government proposals, he had ideas on how to increase the company's chances of success the next time around. In addition, the candidate had a friend who already worked at the company, so he knew a little bit about the department manager's style. He knew Chris was an avid Redskins fan and took the opportunity to chat about last week's game. Chris was very impressed and in the end, she hired him. The other interview that stood out to her was another candidate who had done his research, but instead of using the information that he had gleaned from his research to build rapport, he used it to do the opposite. When Chris asked this candidate what he had done to prepare, he began to list all the details he had learned from his research, including Chris's recent divorce and house purchase, how much the house had cost, and the fact that the school district would be great for her son. The candidate knew that Chris had moved from a town in Maryland and what high school and college she had attended. Needless to say, Chris was more than a little startled and turned off. Both candidates clearly did their research. Both had extensive knowledge about the company and how they would best fit in. The first candidate had probably stumbled upon public records or blog postings and thus had access to the same information as the second candidate, but he used this information to build rapport without seeming like a stalker. Just because you know something doesn't mean you should use the information! Perhaps the second candidate could have built rapport with Chris by mentioning his struggles with his own recent house purchase instead of saying that he knew she had just bought a house. Chris would have probably felt a sense of rapport because she, too, had just bought a house and thought it was a neat coincidence. The second candidate didn't use his knowledge to his advantage; instead, he used it to intimidate and alarm, and thus destroyed his chances of getting hired. And because HR professionals from different companies talk frequently, he probably ruined his chances at many other government contractors, as well. We will go into more detail in Chapter 5 on how to approach a target for professional gain.

Image Management

Now that we have learned how to conduct recon, baseline, build rapport, and make contact, it is time to flip that around: Other people are also doing the same to you. When you go for an interview or on a date, you can be certain that recon has been done on you. It is extremely important that you know what they are going find and that, if you need to, you can clean up your online persona.

Creating a brand

The first step in controlling your social media persona is to determine what you want your "brand" to be. I don't mean in the sense of a corporate brand. What I mean is determining how you want the world to perceive you—you as the total package. Do you want to be seen as a hardworking, well-respected attorney with many important connections who is also a mother of two? Do you want to be seen as an expert in fashion? Remember, you don't want to become so worried about how you appear that you become Stepford versions of who you think you should be. You don't want to come off as boring or having nothing to contribute. You want the world to see your unique personality shining through as you create content that supports and augments your brand. This is not a book on branding; there are a lot of great resources that can certainly teach you how to better define and build your brand, but for our purposes, we can do this by answering a few simple questions

- In a few words, what makes you unique?

- How do you want others to see you?

- What would your catch phrase be?

Take some time and really think through the answers to these questions. By piecing together your answers, you will be able to start fleshing out your brand. This is not a static thing: You can change your brand if you decide that you want to show a different side of yourself. We are constantly going through changes as we get older or move up the career ladder or have other life events affect us.

Now that you have figured out your brand, you have to work with it.

Highlighting different facets of your brand

A well-known fashion blogger once told me that after you figure out your brand, it is important make sure that you remain consistent in your brand across all social media outlets. This is true, to an extent. You will play up different sides of your brand on certain outlets than you would on others. A brand is typically a few words that define you—for example, "intelligence social media expert" (that's mine). However, because we are people and not products, there are many facets to our brands, meaning there are many parts of our personalities and our lives that make us who we are.

For example, I am, variously: a cyber intelligence branch chief, a teacher of social media image management and protection, a friend, a wife, an adoring dog owner, a horseback rider, a computer geek, a Junior League member, a lover of reality television, a lover of restaurants, and a fashion trend follower. I am all of those things and more, and they all go into making me who I am. Together, these facets make up my personal brand, even though my professional brand is "intelligence social media expert." Accordingly, I will lean more heavily on and talk more thoroughly about different facets of my brand based on the social media outlet that I am using. I will also be more cautious in my presentation of content with some social media outlets than with others. There is a time and a place for everything. I would not go to a wedding in shorts and flip-flops, nor would I go to the beach in a business suit. I would never discuss the personal problems of a friend with my boss at work, nor would I discuss my work to-do list with close friends at Sunday brunch.

You change your attire, content of speech, and sometimes even facets of your personality to blend with your environment. The same applies for the different social media domains. For example, I would never post about my dog on LinkedIn because I use it only for professional connections and content. LinkedIn is a professional networking social media site; therefore I will show only the professional facet of my brand when using it. However, Facebook is more personal, so I feel free to post content about my dog or other personal aspects of my life. The same applies in reverse: On Facebook, I would not discuss details of work because it is not the right place.

A few rules of thumb:

- Pinterest, Instagram, Facebook: more personal in nature.

- Linkedin and other professional networking sites: keep it professional.

- Twitter: both professional and personal, depending on your goals.

Part of having a brand is the brand recognition that comes with it. Anywhere in the world you go, you know what the Golden Arches mean. Similarly, it's important for you to use the same name for all of your various social media outlets, so that people can find you on Instagram, Twitter, Facebook, LinkedIn, and more, simply by typing your name into Google. The style blogger I mentioned previously told me that if you go against your brand or do not remain consistent, people will get confused or disenchanted, lose interest, and move on. Because my blogger friend makes her living with her brand and blog, she is has to be very conscientious about remaining consistent. Admittedly, most of us are not professional bloggers, but it is still important to remain consistent in your brand as a professional and an expert in your field. Once you have followers, you want them to remain interested in what you have to have to say.

Social media is an interactive experience. When people make comments or ask questions, you have to respond quickly. People have short attention spans and will lose interest if they don't get a response within a day. My blogger friend recommends responding to a specific question within 24 hours; if she can't, she will typically write a much more detailed and heartfelt response to apologize for not getting back to the follower quickly. She recommends that if you want to keep followers, set aside an hour or two each day in the morning or evening to answer questions or respond to comments. She said that it's important to update your blog or posts daily. Again, if people get bored with or confused by your image, they will move on.

So how does this apply to us in the business or social world, where we probably aren't bloggers? We can take the blogger's advice and apply it to a normal business professional using social media:

- We want to create our own image and brand so others don't do it for us.

- We want to stay consistent with our image and brand by posting things that match that image.

- We want to respond to questions on our social media in a reasonable amount of time, usually within 24 hours.

Waiting 48 hours to respond makes you look lazy and uncaring. People following you in your professional field expect professional courtesy. If you are trying to get the attention of an expert or senior in your field, she messages you on a social media site, and you wait a few weeks to get back to her, you can consider that contact gone. She will have moved on and you will have lost the contact, most likely forever.

Removing negative content: pitfalls and perils

Part of image management is controlling your content. We have all heard the saying that everything posted on the Internet is there forever. That is mostly true. Even if you delete a picture, a posting, or a response to blog, there is no guarantee that the content will ever be fully removed. Others can download it, and the Wayback Machine or some other time capsule site can capture and store it. So if you cannot ever totally remove something from the Internet, how can you clean up your online persona? Sometimes what you want removed is not even something that you yourself posted. Maybe a friend posted and tagged an unfortunate picture of you from a bachelor party, or maybe someone made a negative comment about you or your business. Businesses live and die based on their reputations, and one really bad Yelp review can hurt a business's bottom line for a long time. I will not go to a restaurant if I read even a single bad review about it, and I typically won't purchase a product if the reviews are bad. These reviews may or may not be factual, but most people still heed them nonetheless.

Our personal reputations are just as important and crucial to our success. We are often more likely to believe third-party praise about another person rather than we would if we heard it from the person him- or herself. If a friend claims he is great and skilled at cooking, I tend to believe him. But if I were to hear that he is a great chef from someone else, I will believe it even more. So, what do you do if your personal reputation is in jeopardy due to negative content that you posted, or that someone else posted about you? Most people automatically assume that they just need to have Google or some other search engine remove the content, but that is not exactly how it works. When you use Google or another search engine to look for content, understand that Google is just sending you to the original content or a cached version of the content. (*Cache* is content that is saved so that you don't have to be sent to the original document each time; eventually it updates and expires.) The Google search engine does not maintain original content, unless you are using Google Hangouts, a different service than the search engine, in which case Google does house the content. So if you want to really and truly remove something, you need to go to the source, which is the Website hosting the information you want removed. This could be a blog hosting platform, such as Tumblr, a specific individual Website, or a social media site.

There are many problems with this approach. First, the Website or blog likely owns that content, according to the terms of service. This means that the site is under no obligation to remove it. If you didn't post the content that you want removed, you might have a better shot with the content host by nicely and persistently asking them to remove it. The next difficulty is that you might have a very tough time finding the right person to talk to get the content removed. Anyone who has ever been on the phone with the DMV knows how frustrating and disenchanting this can be. Added to this issue is the language barrier you'll encounter if the blog or

Website isn't hosted in the United States. Some content might be easier to get removed than other content. Even if you were lucky enough to find the contact information for the original site and to get them to remove the content, understand that there is no way to control who else might have downloaded and redistributed it before it was removed. For example, if you post an image and later want it removed, you might get lucky and be able to get the hosting site to remove the photo. All the search engine caches will eventually expire, and the content that was linked to that site will eventually disappear, as well. But how do you know that 100 people haven't already downloaded and posted that picture on their own sites? You can use Google Image to search for it, and maybe you will be lucky enough to locate all of the pictures, but now you have to try to get all of those *other* people (and their friends, who probably copied and downloaded it, too!) to remove it. It is an endless cycle. Chances are, a time capsule site will not remove the content. The simple answer is you really can't guarantee removal of any content from the Internet with 100-percent certainty. The exception to this would be illegal content. Illegal content or content that has to be removed due to a court order (and which is hosted in the United States) will be dealt with differently; we will go into that in Chapter 7. But if you can't really fully remove most content, what can you do?

That is where "reputation cleaner" companies such as Reputation.com come in. Social media reputation cleaners have hit the market en masse. These companies do not actually remove negative content; they just bury it so that is harder to find. Most people who Google you will only look at the first 20 results or so. Reputation cleaners put newer, more positive content toward the top of searches so that most people will not find the negative content, which is now buried further down the search results. These services will also actively search for negative content about a client. We can only spend so much time researching our online identities for negative comments or posts. Like credit monitoring services, reputation cleaners monitor your online persona and reputation, and alert you if they find something suspicious or deleterious. These are good services to use to keep your reputation clean. That said, it is always better to prevent a problem from happening in the first place than it is to try and fix one that already exists.

- - -

Now that you have a better understanding of social media and how to use it to baseline, conduct recon, build rapport, and make contact with a target, let's move on to using social media in the professional domain and how to best portray yourself there.

}-(((*>   **5**

Using Social Media
for Professional Gain

<*)))-{

Digital forensic examiners are often called upon to act as expert witnesses during court cases when the cases they work go to trial. A digital forensic examiner colleague of mine was called upon to testify as an expert witness. He was a very good forensic examiner and well regarded in his field. He had a great professional reputation. When he got on the witness stand, the defense attorney asked him to state his profession. The examiner answered that he was a forensic examiner with the Department of Defense. The defense attorney asked him if he was sure. The forensic examiner replied that he was. The defense attorney again asked him to please state his profession. Annoyed, the forensic examiner replied that he was indeed a forensic examiner with 12 years of experience who worked for the Department of Defense. The defense attorney held up a printout of the forensic examiner's social media page. He turned to the courtroom and the forensic examiner, and asked for him to explain why, if he was a forensic examiner, his profession was listed as "pimp to all the ho's" on his social media site. As you can imagine, this threw the forensic examiner off. Not only did people laugh at him, but his credibility was completely shot. Clearly, maintaining a positive professional reputation and image is critical to the future of your career. As we discussed in the previous chapter, it can make all the difference in whether or not you are hired, receive promotions, or are respected in your field. Just one mistake like this one can have grave consequences to your professional success, now and far down the line.

It bears mentioning here that the First Amendment (the right to free speech) does not protect your "free speech" from the private sector, only from *government* interference. If you work for the private sector, an employer has the right to fire you (or not hire you) for anything that you have posted or anything found in your online persona.

According to a *Time* article:

A new survey released by Jobvite, a company that provides applicant tracking software, shows that 92% of employers are using or planning to use social networks for recruiting this year. This is up slightly from last year at 89%. The study retrieved insights from over 1,000 companies, mostly based in the U.S., in a wide variety of industries. Even if you don't supply a recruiter with your social network profiles, 73% of recruiters will check them out anyway.[1]

You represent your company even when you're not on the clock. Most companies have a morality clause and can and will fire you for posting content that portrays you or them in a negative light. When posting, always remember the rules you learned in Chapter 2. Take the time to really think about how each post will be perceived as part of the whole. Not only does it look bad to your employer if you are posting offensive or inappropriate content, but it also looks bad to other professionals in your industry, which in turn affects your future career prospects. If your professional community has a negative perception of you, you will not be respected or taken seriously.

All of us have known or worked with someone who badmouths his colleagues, boss, or job. Never discuss negative things about your work on your social media. Not only do you run the risk of getting fired, but you may also turn off future employers or experts who could help you in your field. Every HR professional I talked to for this book stated that if they saw someone badmouthing his work, colleagues, or boss, they would not hire that person, even if they were familiar with the company the person was complaining about and felt that the complaints were justified. Remember, it is one thing to complain in private and in person to your close friends, family, and support system about work; it is something else entirely to post it for everyone to see. And *never* use profanity while talking about your work, or online in general.

What Recruiters and Professionals Want to See—and What They Don't

From the *Time* article mentioned previously:

What are they looking for? First off, it's important that you have profiles on LinkedIn, Facebook and

Twitter. If you don't, you won't seem as relevant and companies might think that you're hiding something. Next, companies are inspecting social profiles to weed out candidates and to get a sense of whether a particular applicant is likely to fit into the culture or not.

What you post or Tweet can have positive or negative impact on what recruiters think of you. Four out of five recruiters liked to see memberships and affiliations with professional organizations on a candidate's profile, and another 66% react positively when a profile mentions volunteerism efforts. On the other hand, references to illicit drugs, posts of a sexual nature, and mentions of alcohol consumption were likely to be viewed negatively by 78%, 67%, and 47% of recruiters. Interestingly enough, poor grammar and spelling mistakes are worse social networking sins than writing about your latest binge-drinking adventure: 54% of recruiters had a negative reaction to grammar and spelling mistakes, compared to 47% of recruiters negative reaction to alcohol references."[2]

When I asked HR professionals, they confirmed that these statements were true. If it looks like you don't know how to use social media, you are viewed as either hiding something or irrelevant. As I mentioned in a previous chapter, if you are one of those poor souls who does not believe in punctuation and you are over the age of 15, get in the habit of using proper grammar and mechanics. Yes, there is a mode of expression that is accepted in text messaging and informal social media circles, but to maintain a good impression, use this language sparingly. There is a big difference between using abbreviated words or text message language such as "lol" or "OMG" or "totes amazing" in a personal context, with friends and family, versus in a professional setting. You want to train yourself to become the person who can turn it on and off at will, depending on the context. Recruiters and employers care very much that you are able write and speak like a professional and will check all of your social media, not just the professional sites.

My friends L and M recently had a beautiful baby girl. L decided to use an online site to begin to interview potential babysitters. She posted an ad on a respected Website where babysitters who have been through a screening process post their online profiles. In response to L's ad, a potential babysitter posted this response (I have changed some words to protect the identities of the people concerned):

I would have a background check on me but I'm having issue with the whole credit card thing but I'm willing to be completely honest with you as far as your children's safety and wellbeing but I would love to be a nanny for your kids and take the class well if employed because I'm not making much at my current job and desperately want to quit and do something I'm passionate about also I'm looking for a career opportunity, I'm only working part-time and this is a great jump start into my career choice plus i love working with children and this would be a great choice to establish myself while bringing you a highly motivated person and started babysitting while attending middle school, i provided both before and after care during the school year. During the summers

I provided all day child care for friends and relatives, Im also CPR and FIRST AID certified as well i also worked in a daycare for 3 months before so can really want to work for you so please please give me a chance i really need a job and i need to help my sister with bills as soon as possible.

Regardless of the credit background check issue she brings up, notice the lack of correct grammar and spelling. Everyone polled said that if someone can't even take the time to write a professional-sounding ad with proper grammar, punctuation, and spelling, imagine the lack of attention she would have when watching someone's child. One even stated, "I can't think of anyone who would read this and want to hire this person to watch after their children." The nanny wannabe in this advertisement might be the best and most professional nanny out there, but based on her e-mail and content posting, she will be perceived as unprofessional and inattentive, and thus probably won't be able to find anyone who will hire her. The lesson here is to check and double-check your professional e-mails and any posted content. Otherwise, you'll be selling yourself short and shooting yourself in the foot.

Making Your Professional Image Work for You

People who simply do their jobs well do not necessarily get ahead anymore. According to Paul, a former VP at a Fortune 100 company:

You have to create a buzz about yourself and do your own public relations, because no one is going to do it for you. But you have to be careful. You need to let your boss and others know the good things that you are doing without sounding conceited. Using social media is a great way to do that.

I have been in the digital forensic community for a long time and have a long and solid list of professional connections. I have had a very successful career and am considered an expert on cyber topics. However, I didn't start off that way. I had to work hard to prove myself and get my name out there. If I hadn't created my own buzz, no one would have known about me or considered me to be the professional that I am. To help establish myself in the cyber community, I made sure that my professional social media profile branded me as a digital forensic examiner specializing in cutting-edge forensics. I made sure my profile had all the right buzzwords. I followed many well-established and respected bloggers in the community and got to know them. I followed many online forums related to forensics. I friended a lot of heavy hitters in the industry, and asked for and got career advice. I used social media to establish mentors. I became involved with one of the biggest computer security conferences in the industry, called DEF CON, and became personal and online friends with well-known people in the community. After they saw my presentations I began to get endorsements from them as well as from colleagues and seniors based on the results of my work. I spoke at conferences and made sure to post to social media such as YouTube and relevant forums. I wrote a forensic textbook, which I also posted on my social media pages. I created the image that I wanted people to see, but there was substance behind the image. You have to actually be able to back up your online persona and brand. You certainly can't claim to be an expert in something if you are not. It is critical to your success that you self-promote using professional social media sites such as LinkedIn. You could be the best at what you do, but if no one knows about it or if you don't promote yourself, it isn't going to help you advance your career or give you more opportunities.

However, this is a tricky line to walk. The trick is learning to promote your expertise and successes without appearing arrogant. Not only is it critical to promote your successes, it is important that you associate with other professionals who can validate that you are successful and back up your expertise. Obviously if you are just starting out your career, you will not be considered an expert and should not promote yourself as such. However, you want to show your successes and let your professional community see you as a hardworking go-getter who will be an expert at some point. Remember that you are also defined by who you know. Use this to your advantage. If you have links to well-known, highly placed people in your industry, ask them to endorse you and by all means show that they are your connections. Having these experts as connections shows your boss, seniors, hiring managers, and other experts that you have connections with experts in your work community and that you are taken seriously by them. This gives you clout in your employer's eyes.

I was interviewing for an engineer to join my team. I knew his name and had heard good things about him. I did my recon on him and was blown away not only by the powerful and expert connections that he had on his LinkedIn profile, but also by the endorsements of his skills by experts. In the end, that became the deciding factor in choosing him for the job.

Using Social Media to Get Expert Help

It is not enough to have a great professional social media profile and good connections; you have to actually use them. To get yourself out there and remain on the radar and keep up to date in your field, you must use social media to follow important organizations in your professional area and make comments on topics that interest you. Make yourself known. You want to follow industry leaders in your field on Twitter and LinkedIn. Remember that if you look at someone's profile, he or she will most likely look at yours, too. Use this to your advantage. By commenting on and/or re-Tweeting their posts, people who you admire can essentially get to know you. By using these media, we have immediate access to senior leaders and experts in our chosen professions. Do not be afraid to reach out to them and ask questions. If there is a person whom you admire in your field, follow him or her on social media. Do your research and recon and eventually you can use this medium to build a rapport and even ask the person to mentor you or assist you in advancing your career. Make sure you list your accomplishments. Your boss may have no idea that you wrote a book or published a paper a few years back or are actively involved with an admirable charity or professional association. Maybe your boss will see that you headed your charity's fundraiser. Your boss might then see that you have experience in leadership and give you more respons-ibility or a promotion based on your outside experience. You want to present an image of yourself as a well-rounded person. Remember that their perception of you based on your online persona is _their_ reality of who you are. Stay away from joining organizations that the people you are trying to impress would deem inappropriate. As we saw in the *Time* article quoted earlier in this chapter, HR professionals like people who are well-rounded and who have hobbies. To look well-rounded, it is important to have hobbies. I don't recommend that you post about your hobbies to strictly professional social media, but I do encourage you to do so on personal social media such as Twitter or Facebook. If you love to cook, talk about cooking. If you do charity work, talk about that. Join all of your company's social media accounts and follow them to keep up to date and current on the latest technologies, trends, and happenings. Find professional organizations that are respected in your field, follow them, and repost and Tweet about them. HR professionals and other experts will seek out your non-professional social media. All of the HR professionals that I interviewed felt that they get a better sense of who a person is by following their non-professional social media sites than they do by actually talking with them. I believe this is true, and so I highly recommend that other HR professionals use both personal and professional social media to get a real sense of a person and his or her fit within a company. Without giving away any trade secrets, and with your company's permission, post helpful tips that you have learned in your job that others can learn to show that you, too, are an expert in your field.

Even though you have friended experts and made sure that your professional profile is strong, with your accomplishments listed and plenty of endorsements to back them up, you won't be able to succeed just by yourself. Everyone needs a bit of help from others to get to the next level in their career and to succeed professionally. With social media, as I stated previously, you have instant access to many people with whom you would otherwise never have any contact with. If you successfully build rapport with them, most professionals will want to help you. The best tip for getting people to help you, including strangers, is to actually *ask* for their help. It really is that simple. Sure, it can be scary putting yourself out there, and you probably will encounter rejection, but if you don't ask, you definitely will not get what you want. You have to know exactly what you want, and exactly how people can help you. Then you need to craft a message or e-mail that quickly gets to the point. You want to be humble but confident. Recon on your target is crucial. By knowing a little about your target, you can tailor your message to something that would make her want to respond. For example, if your target person is passionate about a topic, make your message show that same passion. If your target seems to have a dark sense of humor, allow your message to contain a similar, but subtle humor. Use language that she uses. Never send out a mass message to multiple people whose help you are soliciting. You must always tailor your message to each individual person. The same tactic will apply later in the chapter on online dating.

I knew nothing about the trade publishing industry when I first began the process of working on this book. My prior experience was limited to the very different world of textbook publishing. I felt that I had an important message and wanted to get it out to the general public. Even though I had published textbooks prior, I had no idea what to do to find a trade publisher or even where to start. I began doing research on trade publishing using the Internet. I learned about how to contact literary agents and publishers. I learned about the format of the query letters that had to be written. I began sending out query letters and found myself either getting rejections or no response at all. I knew exactly what type of publisher that I wanted to target but I also knew that I was doing something wrong. I just had no idea what it was. I turned to social media. I used LinkedIn and began searching for experts in the trade publishing industry. What I needed was someone who would look at my query letter, tell me what I was doing wrong, and offer his or her advice. I found two experts who I felt might be able to help me. I did recon on both so that I knew a bit about them. One had a very good sense of humor, so I tailored my message to him using his style of humor. The other was very serious and to the point. She had been in publishing for many years and knew the lay of the land. I tailored my message to her using a serious, businesslike tone. Both messages were to the point and only a few paragraphs long. I made sure to state who I was, what my goal was, what I had done to achieve my goal thus far, and why I felt that each was the right person to help me. Both responded to my message within a few days. They not only took the time out of their busy schedules to talk with me, but they also read my query letter. They both had great advice and suggestions for me. Using their advice, I was able to find the perfect publisher. I went from knowing nothing about trade publishing to knowing exactly what to do.

If people do help you, it is critical that you thank them and let them know how much you appreciate their taking the time to help you. I thanked them both and updated them on my status. I keep in touch with both. I know that without their help, I might not have gotten to where I am today. But I also know that if I hadn't asked in the first place, done recon, and baselined them to build rapport by writing tailored message to them, I would have never gotten their help at all, and thus I might never have found the perfect publisher.

Smarter Social: Thinking Outside the Box

Crowdsourcing is the process of soliciting small contributions from the general public. For example, many successful diets work by crowdsourcing. You tell a group of people what you are eating for the day and they help plan a menu or offer comments on what you are eating. Because you feel accountable to the people helping you, you are more apt to stick to the diet. Here's another example: The average research scientist deals with an 80-percent grant rejection rate. To get a government research grant, you have to go through an arduous process that usually does not succeed in securing a grant. Ethan Perlstein, a researcher, wanted to get $25,000 to do research on how methamphetamine affects the brain.[3] He felt that chasing government grants to undertake research took a long time, and also created a separation between science and the general public. So he decided to crowdsource to get the money he needed. He created an online pitch in which told the public what his experiment was and the benefits it could offer. He offered to upload regular updates for the public to see. In the end, by using crowdsourcing, he was able to secure the $25,000 he needed for his experiment. Like Ethan, you can use social media in a creative manner to get the things that you want, such as a grant, perfecting a white paper, or getting a new job. A job search can be overwhelming. But with your LinkedIn and other social media sources, you have an excellent trusted network of potential employers and referrals right at your fingertips. By asking your friends and former colleagues to help you and querying your network of people (who already know what a great employee you are), you have a great shot at landing a new job.

A while back, a system administrator just starting his career looked me up on LinkedIn. He told me that he had followed my career and was interested in getting a job as a forensic examiner. He was in the computer security field. I was impressed that he took the initiative to reach out to me. He passed along his resume and asked me for tips on what I thought he should do to make the jump from computer security to forensics. I suggested that he begin to promote himself on social media for his work in security and frame it so that he would get the attention of forensic professionals. I advised that he friend me and some other known experts in the community on social media, and that he take some classes in forensics and learn the buzzwords and jargon. I suggested that he join some forensic associations, and start reading some of the blogs and attending conferences. After a while, he became more ingrained in the community by using his online profile to get what he wanted. He is now working as a forensic professional for a large government contractor and is creating a good name for himself. If he had just tried the traditional path of taking classes and applying for jobs without references and without using his online identity to enhance his image, he would not have made the jump into the forensic community as quickly and as seamlessly as he did. Of course you should never lie and say that you have done something that you haven't, but you can always model your online identity after experts in the field you are trying to get into, just as this system administrator did.

The beauty of using social media is that you can gain access to experts in a way that you never could in the real world. Many people, including experts, are good and decent people, and if they are approached in the right way, they will likely be flattered and want to help you. Don't be afraid to send friend requests to experts in your field and ask for assistance or advice. The worst thing that can happen is that they ignore you or say no. Read their profiles and do your recon and baselining before you approach them. You want to send out your requests in way that shows that you are respectful of their time and want their advice. If you do this correctly, you will have success more often than not.

Connecting Using Photos

Using photographs of yourself is a good way to put a face with a name. Having a photograph personalizes you to other professionals. If you are using photographs to propel your professional image, you do not want to use inappropriate images where you are engaged in non-professional types of activities (like that awesome photo of you dancing on the bar after one too many tequila shots—remember that one?).

There are some other good rules of practice for posting photos to professional social media sites that might not be as obvious. Don't use an action shot, such as you finishing a marathon or skydiving. Sure, it shows that you have a great hobby, but people want to see your face. Keep the action shots to personal social media such as Facebook. Also, do not use a photo of your dog as your professional photo. You want a clear shot from the neck up, in which you look clean, professional, approachable, and happy. Don't use a blurry photo or one in which any part of your face is hidden. And don't wear a hat. If you follow these rules, the sky's the limit, and building your buzz is 100 percent within your control.

> ### *What Looks Professional*
>
> - *Being well-rounded.*
>
> - *Having expertise and a good professional social network, including experts and seniors.*
>
> - *Friending your company.*
>
> - *Creating buzz.*
>
> - *Writing an industry blog or white paper.*
>
> ### *What Counts Against You*
>
> - *Repeated references to drugs or alcohol.*
>
> - *Constant complaints against your boss or job.*
>
> - *Bad grammar and spelling or cursing.*
>
> - *Showing immaturity; engaging in "flame wars."*
>
> - *Connections to unsavory or unprofessional people or groups.*
>
> - *Lies.*

Lying Online Is a Big No-No

In a *Seinfeld* episode, Elaine lies to her boss to get out of work by saying that she has to take care of her sick father, but instead goes to a baseball game with George and Kramer. A confrontation in the stands ensues, and her picture ends up in the sports section of the newspaper. She fears that her boss will see the photo and know that she lied. We have all heard stories of someone who calls in sick and then runs into his boss at lunch or in some other compromising place. The same is true for social media. As we now know, most social media sites by default will show the location you are posting from and the time of your posts. I am by no means advocating that you call in sick to go to a baseball game, but remember that date and time stamps can show where you were at a certain time. Most of us would probably not post photos of ourselves at a baseball game if we had called in sick to work, as Elaine did in the *Seinfeld* episode. However, it is never a good idea to lie because even though you might not post your transgressions, someone else might! A former work colleague once told me a story about an employee on his team whom we'll call John. John and some of his colleagues were at a conference in Las Vegas for work. John's responsibility was to attend the conference and report back on the presentations he had attended. His trip was paid for by his company. John came back from the conference and turned in his report on the trip. My former colleague thought that the write-up for the second day (Tuesday) of presentations was rather weak and missing detail. He let it go. Another member of his team came to him a few days later and told him that one of John's Facebook friends had tagged John in a photograph at a bar during the conference drinking out of one of those tall "hurricane" drinks that can only be found in New Orleans and Las Vegas. The caption the friend posted read: "So hammered that John ended up in bed all Tuesday hugging the toilet bowl. Way to go John." John had clearly missed Tuesday's presentations because he had partied too hard the night before. Even though John didn't post about it, a friend did, and because John was Facebook friends with his other coworkers, someone saw it and turned him in.

This story drives home some major lessons, the first being that you cannot get away with lying in today's world of social media, where everyone's phone turns them into a film director and you into an accidental YouTube star. The second point is that the real world and the virtual world are merging. Just like John in this story, things that you do in the real world are now showing up on the Internet.

When the Physical and the Virtual Collide

We have all gone on horrible dates. We have all probably done things that we are ashamed of and don't want the world to know about. Perhaps you went to that bachelor party, had one too many tequilas, and thought it was a good idea to dance on the bar or get into a fight, or something else scandalous that you wouldn't want to be forever viewable by anyone searching your online identity. You're probably thinking, *Well, one small bad choice won't forever tarnish my professional reputation or that of my employer. And thank goodness that I can still safely go to bars or restaurants and not have everything I do uploaded on the Internet for everyone to see, right?* Wrong. Aside from the fact that nowadays everyone has a camera on them at all times, webcams are popping up in bars and restaurants. One such service that does this for establishments is Gobeforeme.com.[4] Gobeforeme.com places webcams in bars and restaurants so that you can see what's going on there before you venture out. The theory is that this will help people decide where to go based on what their intentions are. Let's say you are looking to go to a bar to meet girls. You use Gobeforeme.com and see that there is no one at the bar you were thinking of going to, so you keep looking until you find one that looks suitable for picking up girls. Or, maybe you want a quiet place where you and your friends can sit and chat. Gobeforeme.com will help you do that, too. But think about how this affects patrons at these establishments. Suddenly that bachelor party where you had one too many can have real consequences. Do you really want your employer to watch you in an alcohol-induced state? If that doesn't open your eyes, it gets worse. There now exist apps and Websites that enable people to rate their dates, complete with their photographs and full names. Lulu[5] is one such app that enables women to tell stories of men's bad behavior (or sometimes great behavior). It is supposed to be anonymous for the women but not for the men they are "reporting" on. This is just one example of the kind of technology that is out there; more and more are coming out every day. Again, I want to stress that my intention is not to scare you, but rather to inform you that these once separate worlds are now merging, and that things that you do in the real world can now be immortalized for anyone to view on the Internet. You have to be aware of your surroundings and always be thinking about how things that you do can affect your hard-earned reputation.

Words Matter

I have been fortunate in my career to work with some very intelligent and passionate people in both the public and private sectors. Throughout my work, I have been to many conferences. I remember a particular speaker (I'll call her Jane) whom I liked and respected. Based on her presentations, I found her to be intelligent and novel in her approach to her field of study. I had never met Jane in person but was flabbergasted to hear from colleagues of hers that she was not well-respected. In fact, many people used the word "idiot" to describe her. Had these people not seen the same presentations that I had? I didn't know what to think. A few years later, I met Jane at a conference. I introduced myself and asked for her assistance with a case I was working as it was her expertise. When she e-mailed me a white paper, the e-mail message was peppered with such useless and unprofessional words as "like" and "totally," and full of run-on sentences. It was apparent that no spell check or grammar check had been used. There is just no way that you are going to be taken seriously in a professional setting if you write like this. Unfortunately her professional social media was also full of this kind of bad writing. The problem was that she didn't know that this was negatively affecting how she appeared to others. In her presentations I saw a highly intelligent professional, but because she wrote so badly, her colleagues kept her from getting the promotions and respect I felt she deserved.

One final thought on this. It is important that you use words carefully. If you do not know what a word means or how to pronounce it, don't use it. Also, don't use made-up words in regular conversations. I have seen professional social media updates and e-mails filled with phrases such as "he's so romantical" or "she really likes to conversate." Using SAT words in a professional setting or on social media will only get you kudos if you use them properly.

Keep It Concise

I love using more words than necessary when telling a story. I like to pepper my speech with descriptors because I feel that it makes my stories more fun to tell and hear. This works for me in a personal setting when I am with friends and family. However, it does *not* work in a professional setting. In a professional setting you want to come across as confident and knowledgeable. Bosses, colleagues, and clients don't want to read a long, drawn-out narrative. They want to see that you can write in a clear, concise manner that makes sense and states the problem and solution up-front. Personal passion for your work is a good thing, but there is a big difference between using that passion to get an idea across, and looking like you are overly dramatic. Using too many descriptors can distract and bore your audience. Writing for business is very different than writing a book or a letter. When writing for pleasure, we write with our own personal flair and voice. You start with an introduction to get the reader interested, you move into the middle of the story with a conflict or hook, and then finish off with a big finale or denouement. This makes for a good story. It would be ludicrous and boring to try to tell a joke or story where you start with the punch line or give away the ending up-front. However, when writing for business, this is exactly what you have to do. We start with the punch line or point. We use no flowery adverbs or passionate language. State the problem immediately at the beginning in as few sentences and words as possible, and then get to the solution just as quickly and succinctly. I am always surprised by how many business e-mails I receive that have poor grammar, bad spelling, and run-on sentences. Today, many of us frequently communicate with colleagues whom we have never met in person. Most of this communication is done through e-mails, text messages, instant messaging, or social media. When you write for social media and texting, the rules are a little bit more lax, but only a little bit! Your colleagues, bosses, and senior executives are very busy. If you send a long, rambling e-mail, it is almost always going to go unread. When I asked him for e-mail tips, a senior leader at the Department of Defense told me that he routinely ignores e-mails that are filled with too many adverbs. He told me to always make your point in no more than two paragraphs for something important, and just two sentences for something less important. State what you want, how it affects your business, and what the bottom line is. Be clear and concise, and leave nothing open for interpretation. Do not put your politics or opinions in your e-mails. And because you want to be taken seriously, cute or clever e-mail signatures are never a good idea.

Let's look at the following examples:

Dear Big Boss,

I have this great idea that I think will really be awesome for the company. In today's society we are killing tons of trees by printing everything. It is a waste of resources. Someday our children will pay the consequences for our waste. My idea would be really good PR for our company since going green is like a big thing these days. We should stop printing everything and just keep online copies of our paperwork.

Sincerely,
Jane Doe
Manager of Resources
If we don't save the planet, who will?

Mr. Boss,

If the company were to store our TPS reports in PDF format on a file server instead of printing and filing them, the company would save x amount of dollars in printing and paper costs. Also, by storing the PDFs, the TPS reports would be accessible to our customers instantly, instead of having a one-day wait time to sort through files. I spoke with the IT department, which said that there is plenty of storage space on the servers, so the transition would not cost the company anything. I have taken the liberty of creating a simple, 3-step guide to show how to create the PDFs and store them, which is attached for your review.

I look forward to hearing your thoughts.
Very respectfully,
Jane Doe
Manager of Resources

The first example might seem ridiculous, but I have been the recipient of e-mails very similar to it. In the second example, the author did not use the salutation "Dear," as one typically would in personal correspondence. The author has stated her idea in the first sentence and what effect it has on the company. The author has even taken the initiative to talk to IT and create instructions. Which e-mail do you think is more likely to get the boss's buy-in?

One final but very important point: Every industry has its own buzzwords and terminology, and will have expected standards of writing. To fit in with your industry's writing standards, make sure that you frequently read other success-ful white papers or proposals until you learn the expected style of writing and terminology.

- - -

If used properly, your online profile is one of the best ways to promote yourself and build a great reputation in the eyes of potential and future employers, and connect with other experts who can help you get what you want. By using the tips and techniques discussed in this chapter, you will be well on your way to getting ahead in your career, whether it's by using social media or writing a killer proposal.

>‹)))*›   **6**

Online Dating

>‹((((o›

}-(((*›

Many of my friends wonder why they can't find a suitable mate using online dating sites and apps. I have two good friends, we'll call them X and Y, who are also friends with each other. X is a gorgeous woman with a highly successful career. She is funny, smart, kind, and the type of woman I think most men would be dying to date and marry. Y is also smart, funny, sweet, and attractive. However, using the same online dating service in the same city, Y was consistently getting great dates with quality men, whereas X was not. Y eventually ended up in a very serious relationship with a man she had met on the dating site. X came to me and said, "Why does Y keep getting these great men to date, and I keep getting losers who just want to hook up and not get serious, or guys who have no ambition and treat me badly by not calling when they say they will and standing me up?" I decided to compare the profiles of X and Y. Within seconds, I knew why Y was attracting perfect matches for her and why X was not. X's dating profile was all wrong for attracting the type of men she wanted to attract, while Y's was perfect for attracting her perfect mate. I used the tips that you will learn in this chapter to help X write a new profile. Within two weeks, she met a great man to whom she is now engaged. They are one of the happiest and best-matched couples I know.

For this chapter, not only did I rely on my expertise, but I talked to current and past online daters, male and female, ranging in age from 25 to 55. I asked many questions and learned what works and what doesn't. This chapter will reveal tips and tricks for using online dating to help you find your best and most suitable match. At the end of this chapter I will show slightly modified pieces of X's and Y's profiles and let you guess why Y's profile worked and why X's did not, before revealing the answer. This chapter will teach you how to attract the right match for you. In Chapter 10, we will discuss how to vet other people's dating profiles to read what their intentions are, and how to determine deception through their online dating profiles and online personas.

Figuring Out What You Want

There are many dating sites and applications that claim that they will help you find your perfect match. These sites and apps are at various price points and technological levels. There are dating sites that are tailored toward meeting a specific type of person, and more general sites that allow you to filter potential suitors. There are many options to choose from, so how do you begin? The process of online dating will take a lot of time and commitment, so plan to spend at least an hour a day, five days a week on this. The first thing that you need to do is to begin to narrow down what you want in a mate. Are you a single parent in your 30s or 40s who is looking for other single parents? Are you looking for a same-sex mate? Are you divorced and looking for another divorcee? Are you looking for someone from a specific religious or ethnic background? Match.com[1] and e-Harmony[2] are two of the larger, more popular online dating sites. Match.com on its own is a pretty general site; however, it also has off-shoot services, including one for single parents looking to meet other single parents, and a highly technical mobile app that allows you to meet people in real time based on your geocoordinates. With basic Match.com, you fill out a profile, answer some questions, and then search its database of profiles using filters. You can select the people that you would like to reach out to. The site can also match you up with potential mates based on your own profile answers. On e-Harmony you have to fill out a very detailed questionnaire about yourself and what you are looking for in a mate. It uses highly technical mathematic algorithms to match you with people who would be good mates for you, based on the answers to your questionnaire. It is very time-consuming up-front, but saves time in long run because it select matches for you, rather than obliging you to search through hundreds, even thousands of people. I know of many success stories and have attended several weddings of couples who have met using both services. I have also heard many failure stories from both services. There are sites for people looking to meet people of a specific religion, such as JDate.com[3] and Christianmingle.com.[4] There are sites specifically for people over the age of 50. And there are sites geared toward finding a same-sex mate. I think that any of these sites can work for you, but the first step is to narrow down exactly what you are looking for. Once you have determined that, you can begin to target the site or app that is best suited for you. I would highly recommend only using one site or app at a time. As I mentioned, it is a time-consuming process, and if you spread yourself too thin, you will be spending a little bit of time on a lot of sites as opposed to spending a lot of time perfecting and really getting the most out of your one service. If you find that within six months or so a site doesn't work for you, you can always switch. Keep in mind that just because a particular site worked for a friend doesn't mean that it will work for you. You want to pick the site that is right for you and narrow down your criteria as much as possible. The following questions will help you determine what you are looking for in a mate and select which type of site is best suited to help you. Be honest about the answers and write them down:

1. What type of mate are you looking for, physically speaking?

Though I said that the point is to narrow your criteria down, this is the one answer that you want to keep somewhat general. For example, if you typically find yourself attracted to dark hair, you might be getting too specific. When I used online dating sites many years ago, I used the personal filter that I liked dark hair. Had I stuck to that specific filter, however, I would never have met my husband, as his hair is light. Stay away from generalities such as hair or eye color.

All of us probably have a mental image of our personal physical dreamboat, perhaps a certain movie star or other celebrity. When looking for potential matches, understand that you need to be realistic. Using a checklist saying that you are looking for a 6-foot-tall man who is 175 pounds, has blue eyes and brown hair, has perfect six-pack abs, makes a lot of money, and is sweet, kind, and funny, comes from a perfect family, loves his mother, has no baggage, looks exactly like Ian Somerfield, adores your friends, loves all the same things you do, and is the best lover of all time is not at all realistic and just isn't going to happen! It only happens in the movies and in fiction books, so if you are serious about meeting your perfect mate, you have to throw that unrealistic checklist full of ideals out the window. Instead, you are going to have to determine what you can live with and what you can't. This means you'll be narrowing down by deal-breakers. Yes, you want to be attracted to your mate, but some things that you think you *need* might just be things you *want*. For example, your checklist might include a mate who is 6 feet tall, but is it really a deal-breaker if he isn't? Would someone who is perfect for you but is 5 feet 9 inches tall be okay? Most likely, yes. If you want someone who has six-pack abs, would someone who is in just decent shape be okay? Most likely, it would (few guys have actual six-pack abs anyway). The more you narrow down based on superficial things that don't really matter to you, such as eye and hair color, the fewer choices you have to draw from. That being said, don't relax your criteria from wanting a mate with a six-pack to saying that an out-of-shape person will suffice. If you aren't attracted to someone, it's unlikely that you'll have a successful relationship.

2. How old you want your mate to be?

Again, you have to be realistic about this. If you are 40 years old, do you really want to marry an 18-year-old? All the men that I polled for this chapter said that they might select that they would date someone up to 30 years younger on their profile but really they wanted a female mate who was within seven years of their age. For women, most were willing to go 10 years older and four years younger. If you are over 50, there are specific sites where you can meet only over 50s so that you don't have to spend time filtering out people from a general site.

3. *Do you care about your mate's political affiliation?*

Answer honestly. Some people, even die-hard political activists, don't particularly care what their mate's politics are. A married couple that I know couldn't be more politically opposed, but for them it works. They respect each other's political opinions. I will say that even if you are interested in politics and have firm beliefs, do you actually really talk about politics so much that it matters to you? For some people, this is a deal-breaker, and that is okay. Just make sure that you think about it and answer honestly.

4. *What religion, race, or ethnicity do you want your mate to be?*

If this is something that is very important to you, it might be better for you to use specific sites that are geared toward matching people of a specific race, ethnicity, or religion rather than using general sites. If you know that you will not marry someone who doesn't share your religion and you use a general site, you will spend a lot of time weeding out people you would never go out with. But by using a religion-specific site, you know that, at least theoretically, everyone on that site could be a potential mate for you.

5. *What activities do you want your mate to be involved in?*

Are you an avid bicyclist who spends all of your free time biking? If so, you probably don't want a mate who has no interest in bicycles. If you have an activity or hobby that takes up a lot of your time, you might also want to use specific dating sites that will match you with someone with the same hobby, as opposed to using a general site. If you are an active person who wants a mate who is active but don't really have a particular activity that you spend most of your time doing, a general site could work fine for you. You can state that you want someone active as opposed to someone who isn't.

6. *Do you want a mate who wants kids?*

This is important. If someone does not want kids and you do, the chances of him or her changing his or her mind are slim. Cut that issue off early by filtering out people who feel differently.

7. *What about personality type?*

Do you typically gravitate toward the life-of-the-party extrovert, or do you like the more introverted type? Understand that there is not one person who will always be 100-percent introverted or 100-percent extroverted. Think hard about which you tend to be attracted to more. Keep in mind that this might be a good question to get a friend's help with. Even though you always go for the life of party, does that not end up working out? Maybe you are also the life of the party and always end up in conflict, fighting with your mate for attention. When I was dating, I always found my-self attracted to this kind of guy. It was what a thought was a good match for me. A friend pointed this out to me and said that maybe I would be better suited to an introvert instead. If I had been searching for that extroverted type of personality in a mate, I would have missed Matt, who has a more calm-ing personality. Just as my friend suggested, it turns out that what I really was attracted to was a more introverted person-ality. Think honestly about your answer to this question and ask your friends for help. A lot of times we get so caught up in what we think that we want that we aren't able to see things from a different perspective. A friend can see things that you might not be able to.

8. Do you really want a serious relationship?

This is an important question to think through and an-swer honestly. Are you more interested in having a fling than a serious relationship that leads to marriage? Don't say in your profile that you are looking for a serious relationship if you aren't. It is not fair to others who are looking for seri-ous relationships for you to fool them into thinking that you are. It is much better to state exactly what you want or to use the dating sites that are specifically geared toward setting up mates who are looking for flings or non-serious relation-ships.

9. What were the causes of your last few break ups?

Again, be honest with yourself. Get your friends to help you with this. Perhaps they have some insight into the situa-tion that you might not have because you are too emotionally invested. Use what you learn here to keep the same issue from happening in your next relationship. Maybe the answer to this question will tailor the type of mate you are looking for.

- - -

Based on the answers to these questions, you should have a realistic, attainable idea of what you are looking for in a mate. You can also use your answers to narrow down the type of dating site that might work best for you. If you want a more general "catalog" that you can choose from and don't have specific needs, a general site like Match.com or OKCupid might work for you. If you want a general site that will pair you with someone based on a specific questionnaire, or if you don't have time to search through numerous profiles, e-Harmony might be the site for you. And if you are looking within very specific parameters, such as single parents, over 50s, or a same-sex mates only, you will want to use a specific site tailored to exactly what you want. And finally, if you want an "instant" site that links you to people in your area in real time, a GPS-based app service such MeetMoi, OKCupid's mobile app, or Match's real-time app might be your best bet.

Safety First

Now that you have selected a dating site and know what you are looking for in a match, let's go over some safety rules. For any site or app that you choose, you will need to pick a username. Just as you do on professional sites, you want to make a good impression and portray yourself in the best light. If you are looking for a serious relationship but use the username hotsexykitten69, you most likely will not attract the kind of serious mate that you want. Also, do not pick a username that you have used on any other social media site, blog, or anywhere else on the Internet. Remember, you don't want someone with bad intentions to be able to plug in your username and find your social media page that displays personal information about you. For this reason, do not use your real name or any variation of it. Also, you probably don't want HR professionals or other professionals to come across your dating profile. I worked with a very senior professional who used his real name on his online dating profile. Someone at work found the profile and passed it along to everyone on his team. Even though online dating is a good and accepted way to meet matches, it is not anyone else's business. The poor guy was called "likes long walks on the beach" for months.

Along with not using an identifying username and making sure that it is separate from your other social media, do not put any personal identifying information on a dating site. This includes phone numbers, place of business, addresses, your real name, or the names of your children or pets. Even though most people you will come into contact with on dating sites have the same goal as you, there are some really bad people out there who can use this information to hurt you.

Be extra careful with photos. Make sure that any photo you post on a dating site does not have the identifying information, the EXIF data, that we discussed in earlier chapters. Remember that EXIF data contains geocoordinates and other identifying information about the camera that took the photo. *Do not use photographs of your children.* You may certainly say in your profile that you have children if you do, but do not give away any personal information about your children. When I was doing Major Crimes Exploitation of

Children cases, I had a case with a alleged suspected trader of child pornography who, along with having the alleged child pornography on his computer, also had photos of mothers with their children that he had gotten off of dating Websites. He stored them in a folder titled "dating." Remember that anyone who signs up to a site has access to your profile and all the photos in your profile, including your children's photos. We discussed photo-searching applications such as Tineye and Google Image that search the Internet for exact photo matches. *Do not use photos on your dating profile that you have used anywhere else.* Again, we don't want potentially harmful people to find your social media or other sites that have personal information about you.

Discretion Is the Better Part of Valor

When you begin a relationship with someone online, you have the ability to really get to know the person you are conversing with. For example, when Matt and I first met, we lived on opposite ends of the country and used an instant messaging program to get to know each other. I got to know everything about him, and even though we had met in person only once, I felt as if I knew him as well as I knew my best friend. You can feel comfortable with someone pretty quickly through online conversations. However, before you give up personal information and meet the person, have a Skype or other video conversation with him or her first. My friend W was using an online dating site. She had been e-mailing and messaging a man she met on the site for a few weeks. She felt as if she knew him pretty well. However, before they met in person, she set up a Skype call with him. The man she Skyped with ended up being very different from the man she had been conversing with online. He looked the same as he did in his pictures but he was much more aggressive on Skype. When you are e-mailing or messaging online, the other person has time to think of what to say. Tone does not come across as easily in print, so something he is serious about might come off as a joke to you. However, in person or on videophone it is harder because you have to think on your feet. W's friend was aggressive and insisted that they meet. When he had made similar overtures previously over e-mail, she took it as a sign of interest, but when she was able to observe his body language and tone of voice along with his words, she felt threatened. She did not meet him and actually cut off ties with him. Remember that even though you feel you may have gotten to know a person, you only know what he or she has chosen to reveal. *Skype or conduct phone calls before meeting someone in person.*

Another biggie: When you do meet, always meet in a public place. Never go to a private location with a date the first few times. I would recommend this whether you met someone online, at a bar, or at a bookstore. You have to keep safety in mind at all times. You may have heard of the infamous "Craigslist killer." Even though that wasn't result of a dating site, the victims didn't know him and were essentially meeting someone in a private setting who turned out to be a murderer. Along with meeting in public, have a friend know where you are going on your date. I recommend that you do that for any first date, regardless of how you met. And of course, make sure you do a little recon on your potential date using the tricks you learned in Chapter 4.

The Importance of Photos

The people I polled for this chapter unanimously stated that the first thing that they notice about a profile is the photo(s). They also said that they routinely skip profiles that don't have photos. Your photos are going to tell a potential mate a lot about you. That famous saying that a picture is worth a thousand words is accurate in this case. You can post action shots, but you also need at least one head shot of you alone. And men, take note: Every woman I polled stated that if a man wears a hat in every photo, they tend to move on because it looks like he's hiding something. Women and men, if you are insecure about a part of your body or a few extra pounds, don't try to hide it. Every couple I interviewed who met online and are now married or seriously dating stated that what they first noticed about their mate's profile photos was their confidence. Their mate's confidence shined through like a beacon. For men, if you are losing hair, show it proudly and don't try and cover it up. Ninety-five percent of the women polled (including myself) would be more attracted to a man who is losing his hair and shows it proudly and confidently versus someone who hides it beneath a hat (or worse, a bad weave). One hundred percent of men polled stated that they would be more attracted to a woman whose profile photo showed that she was carrying a few extra pounds but was confident and had a great smile, than they would to a woman who had a slim body but looked like she lacked confidence or was not smiling. So, if you are a woman and you are self-conscious about those extra few pounds, get over it and show it confidently!

The next most important thing in a photo is that you look approachable. Men have always complained to me about going to bars and seeing an attractive woman who is in a pack of other average-looking women. They say that they will almost never approach the attractive one because it is too intimidating. Her being a part of such a large group sends a signal, whether she knows it or not, that she does not want to be approached. The same goes for your profile photos. If you are in a pack of your six best girlfriends in every photo, it sends the signal that you're not approachable. It also confuses potential matches as to which person you are. So the best rule of thumb (for both men and women) is to be alone in most of your photos.

This may seem obvious, but don't post photos of yourself with someone of the opposite sex. It could be your sister or brother, but the potential suitor has no idea who this person is and will most likely assume that it is an ex or a current flame, and will move on regardless. We have already discussed not using your children in your dating photos for safety reasons. The same rule applies for showing photos of you with other people's children, such as your nieces and nephews. Not only is it potentially unsafe for the children, because of the lack of control over who has access to the photos, but it confuses your potential mate as to who these children are.

Ninety-five percent of men polled stated that if they saw a profile in which a woman was wearing revealing clothing in every photo (such as a bikini or a very low-cut or short dress), they would view her as a hookup and not a suitable match to date long-term. One guy even stated that, to him, it made the girl look desperate, as though she lacked confidence and was trying to use sex, instead of her personality, to lure a boyfriend. Regardless, if you use all sexy photos, you will not attract the right mate. The exception to this is if you are looking for a fling—then, you are on the right track! One hundred percent of women were equally as turned off by men showing a lot of skin, such as in tank tops or shirtless. One woman stated that there should be some mystery and it made the man appear cocky and self-absorbed if he showed off his abs in even one of his photos.

I know that you love your pet, but do not pose with your pet in every single photo. All of men polled said that it was off-putting, as though the woman were too into her pet. That said, 99 percent of both men and women stated that one photo of someone with his or her pet was a turn-on. (The 1 percent who did not feel this way happen to be terrified of dogs.)

You want to show yourself at your best, doing interesting things. Shots of you doing something such as being on top of a mountain or in Pompeii are great; just don't make all your photos like that. Remember that you want at least one solo head shot. If you are huge tennis fan, show a photo of yourself playing tennis. If you love football, post a photo of yourself wearing your favorite team's jersey. Ninety percent of women polled were turned off by men who posted photos of themselves standing in front of expensive cars or other material objects. Again, it gives the impression of superficiality.

Attracting the Right Person: Do's and Don'ts

I polled a lot of men and women for this chapter. Almost all of them had the same answers as to what turned them off about a dating profile. Let's take a look.

Spelling counts

The number-one pet peeve for almost everyone that I polled was a profile that uses bad grammar and spelling. The thinking is that if you can't even take the time to proofread what you write in a profile, how much time will you really invest in dating? It also makes you look unintelligent. It takes only a few seconds to proofread and run a spelling and grammar check on your profile. It also never hurts to have a friend or family member read it through to find any typos that you might have missed.

| **Don't:** *Make spelling and grammar mistakes.* | **Do:** *Proofread your profile.* |

Mass e-mails

Another huge pet peeve is people who send out mass messages that are not tailored to each recipient individually. It shows the person you are trying to attract that you aren't really serious about dating and are just casting a net to see how many fish you can catch. I know that it is a little more time consuming, but if you are serious about finding a mate, you have to put in the time to respond to each specific message or when first initiating contact, create individual messages to each person. Tell them what you like about them. You don't have to write a thesis. A few sentences are sufficient.

| **Don't:** *Send mass messages.* | **Do:** *Tailor each individual message to the person for whom it's intended.* |

Timeliness counts

Another irritation among both men and women was not responding to messages in a timely manner. This is why I suggest only using one dating site at a time. It is hard to keep up with all of your messages. One woman said, "If we have just started messaging and you wait a few days to respond, it tells me that you are not really interested in me or have too much going on to date." A guy concurred, "How hard is it to take two seconds to write a sentence responding? If a girl doesn't respond, I assume she isn't interested and I move on." Be proactive. Set aside at least one hour each evening to work on your dating profile, at least at first. If you can't get back to someone within a day, have a good reason why.

Don't: *Wait too long to respond to messages.*	**Do:** *Return messages in a timely manner.*

Trying to be someone you're not (aka lying)

Another turn-off for the daters polled was when someone comes across as inauthentic or trying too hard to impress. As you will learn in the next few chapters, your words will say a lot about you and your intentions, and people can usually tell if you are not being genuine, even in a few paragraphs of a profile. If you are not a funny person, don't try to be. Sure, you are trying to market yourself, but just be yourself. One of the men polled told a story about a girl he was interested in who claimed she was a doctor in her profile. She talked about how great being a doctor was and implied that she had the most important job. It seemed weird to him that someone would say that but he ended up meeting up with her anyway. It turned out that she was a nurse, a well-respected profession in its own right. He never contacted her again. He thought, and rightly so, *If she is going to lie about something like that, what else will she lie about?* Most people polled have encountered daters who have lied about their age, weight, or height, or used old photos in which they look different than they actually do. The interesting thing was that people who had encountered this said that people never lied by outrageous amounts. For example, they would add maybe 2 inches to their height, certainly not enough that it would have made much difference. Some people said that they would continue to (and did) date someone who lied by adding or subtracting a few inches, years, or pounds. Some didn't notice, whereas others, like the man who dated the nurse, knew they would not date the person again. For most, it wasn't the substance of the lie itself so much as the question of what else they might lie about.

Don't: *Lie or misrepresent yourself.*	**Do:** *Be truthful.*

Name dropping

Name dropping was brought up a few times so I feel it is worth mentioning. Even if you went to high school with Lady Gaga or once hung out with Paul Ryan, people don't need to know about it. People found name dropping to be annoying. People who drop names don't appear to have much to offer except that they know someone famous.

Don't: *Name drop.*	**Do:** *Make yourself shine just by being you.*

"I like traveling, music, and restaurants"

This phrase, or an equivalent, was brought up a lot. Everyone likes to travel, everyone likes music, and everyone likes restaurants! Both women and men said that they were attracted to profiles in which the person didn't just claim that he or she liked to travel, or listed places that he or she had been, but actually got creative with it. For example, if you say you loved touring the Roman ruins at Pompeii or are passionate about skiing the Alps, that tells your potential suitor that you actually do travel and the things that you like to do when you travel. It makes you seem exciting and adventurous.

Don't: *Use typical language stating that you like something that pretty much everyone likes.*	***Do:*** *Get creative with the things that you've done and the places you've been.*

Boundary crossing

Boundary crossing was an issue brought up by both male and female daters. Like with your professional profile, you don't want to give away too much information. This is not the time or place to tell your whole life story. Remember, you are advertising yourself, and too much information or information that is too personal can be a turn-off. You want to be honest, but you don't have to go into detail. You can say that you are divorced, but there is no need to go into the nasty specifics of your split. And really, you want to have some mystery about yourself and save some things for later.

| **Don't:** Go into specific details and relate everything that has ever happened in your life. | **Do:** Be honest, but keep intimate details to yourself. |

Drama

Many women commented on their annoyance with some male profiles, saying that that they were not looking for drama. One woman stated, "If a guy feels the need to say that he doesn't want drama, there is something behind that and a negative story. No, thank you. I will move on."

| **Don't:** Use phrases like "no drama." | **Do:** Pick your words carefully. |

Checklists

Many men stated that they will automatically move on from a profile that has a checklist of what a woman is looking for. First of all, a checklist is an unreasonable thing to put in a profile. Stating that someone must meet all your criteria is degrading, and makes you look high maintenance and even rude. If you know exactly what you want, you can weed out people by using filters or subtly stating what you are looking for as opposed to a literal checklist of what you must or must not have.

| **Don't:** Use checklists in your profile. | **Do:** Use filters and be open to possibilities. |

Bashing and badmouthing

Lastly, just as you should never bash or badmouth your boss or work in your social media, do not bash or badmouth your exes when you are on dating sites. Everyone polled said that they were turned off by someone who talked badly or said negative things about an ex. It can make you look immature and disgruntled, and as though you aren't over your ex.

Don't: *Badmouth exes.*	***Do:*** *Keep exes out of your profile.*

Putting It All Together: How to Write That Stellar Profile

Now that we have gone over what *not* to do, let's discuss what *to* do. Essentially, you are writing a resume talking about why you are the best candidate for the job of "perfect mate." Many of us have a hard time selling ourselves. This is where you need to rely on your friends to help you with your profile. Ask a friend what he or she thinks are your three best attributes. Ask what qualities you have that the opposite sex is looking for. It is hard for most of us to sell ourselves but that is exactly what you have to do in a dating profile. You need to be willing to write about what makes you great and why you're attractive. Take your friend's answers to the two questions above and think about how you can incorporate their answers into your profile. Not only do you have to sell yourself, but you want to write thinking about your audience, the people—person, really—you are trying to attract and how he or she is going to perceive your profile. Ask your friends of the opposite sex to review and comment on your profile. They might have perspective that you don't.

You want to stand apart from others but also show that you are a normal, well-adjusted person. It is important to show your interests, but you also don't want to give too much away. Save some stuff for later. Show different facets of yourself. For example, you can show that you are into your work but also very interested in a particular hobby. You want to show your potential mate what makes you different and how you stand apart. Even though it might make you uncomfortable, it's critical that you show yourself as the confident, unique, amazing person that you are.

To help drive this home, let's look at the profiles of X and Y from earlier in the chapter and see if we can determine why Y's profile worked and X's did not. I have changed the usernames and modified some of the language to protect the identities of the people involved.

Y's profile: MidwesternGirl2

Y's profile had a great head shot that showed her confident smile. There was an openness and brightness to her eyes. She also had a photograph showing her crossing the finish line of a marathon and one where she was playing with her dog in the park. She also had a full-length body photo in which she was wearing a relatively sexy dress that showed enough but not everything.

Profile:

I am looking for someone to help me take DC by storm. As a staffer on Capitol Hill and recent Midwestern transplant, I feel passionate about my work but also can be found enjoying happy hour at the Pour House, biking the Custis

Trail, or enjoying a nice Sunday walk in Eastern Market. My friends say that I am funny, bordering on hilarious, and often the life of the party, but also, because of my Midwestern values, the kind of girl who people feel that they can always count on and who would never tell your secrets. I am looking for a man whose smile lights up the room because he is often laughing but at the same time can be serious when the occasion calls for it. If you too love biking around DC, talking politics over coffee, don't mind that I will always be a Browns fan, are looking for the perfect mate, and someday dream to hike to the top of a remote mountain, message me.

X's profile: SexyKitten696969

X was dressed provocatively in every photo. In two photos, she was wearing a bikini that left nothing to the imagination. Almost all of her photos showed her surrounded by other girls, with four photos obviously taken in bars. She had a drink in every photo and appeared drunk in a few of them.

Profile:

As you can see I like to have fun and love going out. I am no stranger to happy hours and late nights at Lucky Bar or anywhere in Adam's Morgan. I love shopping and hanging out with my girls. I hate drama and people who lie in their profiles. If you arent 6 feet, don't say that you are. I work to live but defiantly dont live to work. Accountant by day, animal by night. Of you are sexy, single, smart, with a great sense of humor who can drink me under the table or at least try to, hit me back

– – –

Take some time and review the do's and don'ts of this chapter to try and figure out why Y's profile worked and why X's profile didn't.

Answers

Y's profile shows her to be the active, smart, funny girl that she is. The username is perfect for showing an important side of her. The tone is light, but shows that she is looking for something serious without being too grave or dramatic about it. She comes across as smart, funny, confident, and passionate about her work and shows some insight into her value system. Her photos are perfect for attracting a suitable mate's attention. She comes across as cute, sweet, girl next door, and certainly girlfriend and marriage material.

In contrast, X chose a name that is more porn star than girlfriend. Her photos show her as someone she really isn't in reality. You can dress however you want, but if you are trying to attract a suitable boyfriend and/or husband type, you most likely will not attract him with these kinds of photos. Saying and showing that she is always with "her girls" seems at odds with her intention of presenting herself as a suitable mate looking for a serious relationship—if she is always with her friends, when is she going to have time for a guy? Also, the fact that she mentions "no drama" implies that she has had drama in her past, which, again, is sending the wrong message. Her writing has some punctuation and spelling mistakes, showing that the profile was inattentively written and she isn't all that invested in it. Stating that she will only date someone who is "6 foot" makes her appear high maintenance and superficial. There is just no way that this profile will attract the same kind of man that Y's profile will attract, even though their goals were both the same.

- - -

If you take the time to use the tips in this chapter to help you date smarter and more safely online, you are well on your way to finding a suitable match. Take your time and don't get discouraged. Online dating is a process, one that takes diligent effort and hard work. But keep the faith; there are many success stories out there, and yours can be one of them!

Part II

Cyber Judo 101: Protecting Yourself
and Your Family From Predators,
Liars, and Bullies

}-(((*>

7

Keeping Your Child Safe: What You Need to Know

<0))))x

We live in a world where your online reputation is just as powerful and important as the one you have in real life. In fact, they are fast becoming one and the same. We now have the first generation of people whose entire lives are open books available to anyone on the Internet. With this generation, we will have the ability to get information on people from birth all the way through their adult lives. We will have access to an enormous amount of information about them, such as pattern of life, photos, hobbies, phone numbers, marriages/divorces, and the list goes on. Not only is it imperative that we protect our own online identities, but we have to protect those of our children, grandchildren, and other young relatives, as well. In a sense, you have the ability to create their online identities from the day they are born. Most parents post photos of their children, tell stories about them, and provide frequent updates on their lives. Relatives and friends who live far away can see their nieces, nephews, and grandchildren grow up, and feel connected to them in ways that just weren't possible before. This can be a great thing. But you must take special care when posting about children, any children. You need to think hard about what content you are putting out there and whether it is appropriate. The thing to keep in mind here is that you are creating your child's on-line identity, which will follow him or her *for life*. So, what do you want that identity to be?

When you post comments about your children or photographs of them, think about what other people will see and have access to, both now and in the future. We learned about EXIF data in previous chapters. Make sure that photos don't contain any kind of location information. Maybe you took a photo of your new baby in her crib, looking cute in that new onesie that Grandma gave her. Maybe you took a great photo of her at her preschool playing with finger paint, and posted it along with a comment about how great her preschool is. Maybe you post and discuss the things that you do with your child each day, such as reading to her at night. You may be inadvertently giving away her bedtime or other details about her favorite toys or books. Remember, someone who has ill intentions toward you or your child can quickly piece together your location and other sensitive details about you and your child, such as where she lives and where and when she goes to school, and use those details to create a pattern of life for your child. If this ill-intentioned person can learn enough details about your child, he or she might be able to use that information to convince your child that he or she is a friend rather than a stranger.

A detective whom I have remained close with from my days of working child exploitation cases told me a frightening story. He was investigating an alleged child pornographer who was allegedly trading suspected child porn photographs. When the forensic examiner supporting the detective began to go through the potential suspect's computer he found some disturbing chat sessions. The suspect had been chatting with an 11-year-old girl while pretending to be a 13-year-old boy from a nearby school. He claimed that he had met her at a party, even though she didn't remember him. The suspect had gathered a startling amount of information about the girl. He knew where she went to school, where she lived, who her friends were, details about her brother, what kind of dog her family had, when her birthday was, what her hobbies were. He even knew that she was having a hard time at school with a particular girl. She assumed that because he knew so much about her, she must know him and must have met him as he claimed. The girl didn't have a very detailed online profile of her own, so when the detective began analyzing the chat sessions between the two of them, he was unsure how the suspect had gotten so much information about her. He couldn't find any indication that she had given him the specific details that he knew. He began to search online for the girl herself. It turned out that the girl's mother had an open social media site with no privacy settings and frequently talked about her daughter. She was proud of her daughter and thought that she was just sharing things with friends, but lo and behold, because the mother had an open profile with no privacy settings, the suspect was able to learn about the girl and to make her think that he knew her. When the examiner looked through the suspect's computer, he was able to confirm that the suspect had indeed frequently looked at the mother's social media site. Fortunately, nothing happened to the girl, but her mother learned a hard lesson in online protection. Again, my intention is not to scare you into never posting anything about your child, but to make you more aware of the ways in which someone else can use that photo or content to harm you or your child.

Along with not posting personal identifying details about your children, it is also important that that you do not post something that will someday come back to haunt your child. HR professionals are going to have a field day in the future with the vast amount of information available to them on potential candidates. If your child is having a hard time with someone or has done something like skip school, there is no need to post it on the Internet, where it will remain forever. Most parents who do this just want to vent or ask other parents for help, but think of it this way: Would you walk into a room full of your child's potential future employers and tell them all the details about how your son almost got suspended from high school for cheating, or how he always skips school, or that your daughter might have an eating disorder? Would you tell them that your son failed half of his history tests or can't seem to write anything above C-level papers? Because posting these kinds of details on social media with identifying information about your child is essentially the same thing as broadcasting it to any and all future employers. Privacy settings might protect you today, but you don't know what access anyone and everyone might have to your social media in the future. You could potentially harm your child's future career without even meaning to. The Internet has many great private, protected, anonymous sites where you can go and seek help for your child if he is having difficulties, but do not post identifying or private information to your social media. The occasional post about something bad he did is not the end of the world; but remember that his online identity and reputation is going to follow him throughout his life, so you have to manage that identity in such a way that it will foster a spotless reputation, both now and in the future.

Another thing to keep in mind is that the things you post today could make your children direct targets to be bullied later on. That picture of your daughter sitting on the toilet with the caption, "Nancy made her first big girl poo poo" could have disastrous future implications for her when her future school peers find it (and they will!). You can imagine the taunts and the teasing. I know you are proud of your children and want to document and show all your friends and family their milestones, but think about how that photo is going to affect your child later down the road. If you really want to show that photo to someone, send it only to trusted family and friends; do not put it up on social media or the Internet. Or, better yet, save it for when Nancy brings over her first prom date and you bring out the dreaded photo album. You are creating your child's identity and, as a parent, it is your job to make sure that identity is safe and not in any way detrimental to her future.

Now that you have a better understanding of how to manage your child's online identity, do not post photos or details about someone else's child without first clearing it with his or her parents first. If you notice that a friend is posting things about his or her child that you think could backfire on that child, by all means buy him or her a copy of this book!

Keeping Your Teen and Tween Safe

I get nervous when I hear parents tell me that their tweens and teens are so much more advanced than they are about social media and the Internet, and that they have no idea what their children are doing online. There is a fine line that we must walk between keeping our children safe online and letting them have some privacy. It used to be a good rule of thumb to have the computer in a location where you could supervise, but now that most teens and tweens use their smart phones for social media, that is no longer enough. If your child already has a mobile device and social media accounts, the first step is to learn about the programs, apps, and social media that he is using. Ask your child to show you what apps he has on his phone and computer, and what they are used for. You can do a little research of your own, too. Download the same apps, and let your child know that you will be using those apps and that you need him to friend you and give you access to his page. Let him know that you won't comment with embarrassing things like "My lovebug is so cute," but that you need to be aware of whom he is communicating with and what content he is posting. If you are getting your child his first phone and have just begun giving him computer time, you can choose and set up his apps together. Make sure that you have his password but let him know that you do. I personally believe that letting your child know that you have the ability to monitor him is going to work better for you than using spyware or keyloggers without your child's knowledge. However, as a good safety precaution, I do recommend using location apps that will let you know where your child's phone is at all times. These apps allow you use a mapping program to locate your child's phone whenever you need to. Again, I recommend letting your child know that you are doing this. Transparency both ways is always a good idea.

There is only so much that you can do technologically. The most important tip I have is to educate your children on the potential dangers of technology and teach them how to protect themselves. Teach them about EXIF data and the dangers of posting too many details. I recommend reading this and the next few chapters with them to give them the skills and tools they need to make smart choices and protect themselves and their online reputations. Remember, it is a lot easier to prevent a problem than it is to try to clean up a mess. A friend of mine told me a story that illustrates the importance of this. She happened to bring up in conversation that her neighbor had a 16-year-daughter who was always chatting with someone she met online. I suggested that she tell her neighbor about the tips that I recommend in this chapter. The neighbor heeded my advice and began monitoring the daughter's social media. She knew who her friends were, and noticed that something about the "boy" her daughter was communicating with seemed off. Something wasn't right. The "boy" had suggested meeting in person. The neighbor told his daughter to let the "boy" know that if they were going to meet, her father would be tagging along at a respectable distance. Most 16-year-olds would be furious at this, and she was, but she went along with it. The boy immediately cut off contact. Huge red flag! If this had a been a real 16-year-old boy, he would have probably teased her a little bit about her overprotective father, but not thought of it as too big a deal. A person with ill intentions toward the girl would most likely have quickly cut off contact, just as this person did.

Checklist for Keeping Your Children Safe

- *Do not discuss their patterns of life.*

- *Remove EXIF and other location data when posting photos.*

- *Be careful when posting details about your children.*

- *Never post a naked photograph of your child to open Websites such as dating sites or open Twitter, and take care when posting unclothed or partially clothed photos to social media.*

- *Do not air your children's dirty laundry or post content that could affect their future employment.*

- *Do not post photos that could make your children targets for bullying.*

- *Use protection privacy settings on all accounts.*

- *Have your children's passwords to all accounts.*

- *Friend them on all their accounts.*

- *Educate yourself on what programs they are using.*

- *Place tracking software on young children's devices.*

- *Educate your children about safety.*

Cyberbullying: What to Do if It Happens to You or Your Child

We have discussed protecting your children online by doing things that you have some control over, but what do you do about things that you have less control over? According to Bureau of Justice statistics from the U.S. Department of Health and Human Services Cyberbullying Research Center study in 2013, more than 50 percent of students have reported being cyberbullied.[1]

Unfortunately, the news is full of tragic stories about cyberbullying. Most of us have heard the story of Tyler Clemente:

> At college Tyler became a victim of cyber-bullying. His privacy was invaded when his college roommate set up a Webcam to spy on him. The roommate viewed him in an intimate act, and invited others to view this online. Tyler discovered what his abuser had done and that he was planning a second attempt. Viewing his roommate's Twitter feed, Tyler learned he had widely become a topic of ridicule in his new social environment. He ended his life several days later by jumping off the George Washington Bridge. Tyler was eighteen years old.[2]

Another well-known case is the story of teenager Audrie Pott:

> In early September 2012, Pott reportedly went to party with about 10 other teenagers who were allegedly drunk. It is alleged that three or more of these teenagers

raped Pott. During the alleged assault, photographs were taken and distributed via social network and SMS. In the following days, Pott reported being bullied by those who saw the photographs. On 12 September 2012, Pott took her own life.[3]

And then there is the story of Rehtaeh Parsons:

In November 2011, Rehtaeh Parsons, then 15, allegedly went with a friend to a home in which she was reportedly raped by 4 teenage boys. The teenagers were drinking vodka at a small party. Parsons had little memory of the event, except that at one point she vomited. While a boy was allegedly raping her, the incident was photographed and the photo became widespread in Parsons' school and town in three days. Afterward, many in school called Parsons a "slut" and she received texts and Facebook messages from people requesting to have sex with her. The alleged rape went unreported for several days until Parsons broke down and told her family, who contacted an emergency health team and the police.[4]

These stories are horrifying. Bullying has gone on since the dawn of time, but bullying today is so much different than it was when I was a child. Now that bullies have access to the Internet and social media, victims often feel that they will never be able to get away from it. I don't pretend to know what causes someone to bully, but perhaps the feeling of being anonymous online and not having to insult your victim to his or her face contributes to the exceptional cruelty of today's cases of cyberbullying.

Cyberbullying comes in many forms, and it is not just children who are bullied, as the following case proves:

Cheryl Dellasega is a psychologist who also penned a book called *Mean Girls Grown Up*. Dellasega says women commonly attack other women, particularly in cyberspace. "I hear about adult women retaliating a lot more and retaliating in really vicious ways, to the point where sites get shut down, people drop off of sites," she said. This bullying can be one rude comment, or a string of them. It can take place through e-mail, social networking sites, even instant messages. "The topics that women are cyberbullied about are really endless. It could be a romance. It could be your parenting practices," Dellasega elaborated.[5]

How to Identify Cyberbullying [6]

If the bully is:

- *Sending the victim messages that are harassing, filthy, or threatening.*

- *Posting a person's private information online, such as a home address, without his or her consent.*

- *Posing as the victim in order to humiliate him or her.*

- *Posting degrading or humiliating photos or other content.*

- *Sending mass e-mails or text message to a victim.*

- *Hacking a victim's account.*

What can I do?

So what can you do if you or your child or someone you know has been or is a victim of cyberbullying? You can inform the school, but the school may not be able or willing to offer much help:

> When schools try to get involved by disciplining students for cyberbullying actions that took place off-campus and outside of school hours, they are often sued for exceeding their authority and violating the student's free speech right. They also often lose in court.[7]

If you or your child is a victim of cyberbullying, there are a few things you can do. The first is to file criminal charges if the bullying is breaking a law, such as threatening your child with specific intent to harm, or if the bully has broken into your child's account and posted cruel or hurtful content. There are other cases in which you can file civil charges if the bullying does not meet criminal statutes. Different states have different laws. The third option is to notify the service provider hosting the content to get the content or account removed with no intent to file legal charges. The fourth option is to block the bully and get help from organizations such as Bullying.org. The fifth option is, of course, to tell your child to ignore it. Only you and your child can determine whether you want to attempt to file civil or criminal charges. Think through the pros and cons, and work together to come to a decision. Also, talk with other parents who have experience with bullying, with online groups, with an attorney, and/or with your school's guidance counselor or support system. Contact educational organizations such as Stopcyberbullying

.org to help you think through your options and what might be best for you and your child.

Civil vs. criminal cyberbullying cases

Civil cases are generally brought by private individuals or corporations seeking to collect money owed or monetary damages. A criminal case is brought by the local, state, or Federal government in response to a suspected violation of law and seeks a fine, a jail sentence or both.[8]

Depending on the type of bullying and your state's statutes, you can either file criminal or civil charges, depending on which option you have available to you. Anyone can file a civil lawsuit against anyone for anything. If you do end up filing criminal charges, you can also file civil charges. It is not always going to be clear which type of case you have. It is always best contact your local authorities, an attorney, or an organization such as Stopcyberbullying.org to help you determine which charges are applicable in your situation. I am not an attorney and cannot offer legal advice, though I did interview attorneys for this chapter. However, if you or your child is being bullied, I highly recommend that you contact a support system, an attorney, and/or the authorities, no matter what.

Types of Cyberbullying

Sending cruel or threatening messages

Sending cruel, hurtful messages might not meet criminal statues, but could be a cause for a civil case. However, sending a specific threatening message could be considered criminal. In California, the act of threatening falls under Penal Code Section 422. For the threat to be considered criminal, it has to be an immediate, unconditional, and specific threat to commit a crime that will result in bodily harm or death. It must be clear that the bully intended to have it taken by the victim as a threat. Lastly, the victim must be fearful.

For example, if a bully text messages or posts content to a social media site stating that "Jane is a whore," that is most likely not going to be considered criminal. However, "I am going to beat Jane up tomorrow at school at 3 o'clock" is a specific threat and most likely is criminal. Vague threats such as "You'd better watch your back" are not specific enough and would most likely not be construed as criminal.

Posting private information online without consent

This type of bullying may or may not be considered criminal, depending in part on how the information was obtained and what the content is. If the bully finds the victim's address online and posts an ad to Craigslist posing as the victim and states that he wants to be raped at this address, there are statues under which this could be seen as criminal. If the bully is given a photo or an address from the victim that has personal information in it and the bully posts that photo with a caption that reads "A whore lives here," along with the address, it might not necessarily be criminal. However, you may very well have a civil case. If someone posts private medical information that happens to be true without your consent, it may be a federal crime.

Hacking into someone's account to post content

Most likely this will be considered a crime. The bully not only stole the victim's credentials and possibly his or her personal identifying information, but he may well have committed identity theft. He also broke into an account without the owner's permission. This not only is most likely a crime, but it also will violate most terms of service (TOS) of the provider (such as Facebook).

Facelifting

Facelifting is the term for creating a fake Facebook profile claiming to be another person. Many times you won't know that someone has done this. In most cases, someone the victim knows finds it and notifies the victim. A well-known story continues to circulate in the DoD about a Special Forces operator who refused to have a Facebook account. Someone created a profile for him without his knowledge and used it to gather information about him. He had no idea that this profile was out there until one of his friends brought it up. Imagine how much information the facelifter gathered about this guy based on what his friends told him or on associations based on who friended him! Additionally, his friends tagged him in photos, which could have had grave consequences for him, given his profession. In his case, the intent was not to bully. But what if someone were to create a fake page in order to humiliate your child? Again, this could be considered identity theft and could potentially be a crime. Also, the way the bully words the facelifted site might help your case. If the bully uses language on the site in the first person, you will have a better shot at proving identity theft because the facelifter is actually claiming to be his victim.

Posting humiliating content

Examples of this would include "Jane is fat and no one likes her" or "Jane is a whore." Again, a lot is going to depend on the facts to determine whether it is a criminal or a civil case. Most likely something like this would be a civil case, but that can depend on how the content was obtained.

The Crucial First Response

Depending on which course of action you take, there are few things we need to discuss. Your (or your child's) first re-action might be to retaliate or call the bully's parents. First off, never retaliate. You could find yourself or your child crossing a line and end up facing criminal or civil charges yourself. If there is any possibility that you will file charges of any kind and would like to get the bully's account terminated, do not notify the parents of the bully right away. Timing is crucial. Regardless of whether or not you control the content, the first thing you should do is preserve the content. If you control the account, change your password. Do not delete or remove the content, or respond to it in any way. Take a screen capture of the content by holding down the **CTRL** key and pressing the **Print Screen** key on the keyboard. A screen shot will only show an image—it won't preserve the metadata or the content. Next, use a program such as Google Chrome's Webpage Screenshot Capture[9] and choose to save the whole Website with links by saving it as a Web archive. Another tool you can use is ScreenFlow[10] to navigate through the site to capture content. Be careful though: If the content is some-thing like a naked photo of what could be a minor and you download the content to your machine, you could be engaging in illegal activities. If that is the case, immediately contact your local authorities but do not download or capture the page. Take copious notes about the content, such as the time of day of the posting, any location data posted, and so on. Also note the last date and time that you accessed the hacked account legitimately and from what device. Begin to make a list of suspects so that when you inform authorities, you have that information ready.

If you plan to press any type of charges, the next step is to contact authorities right away, if you haven't already. Whether the case is a criminal or a civil case, in some states the authorities will send a *preservation letter* to the hosting Website to preserve all content and metadata about the content, such as IP addresses. Even if the Website is removed or the account is closed, the preservation letter will let the service provider (such as Facebook) know that it needs to keep the data for a potential legal procedure.

If the case is strictly civil, the authorities will most likely suggest you contact an attorney. An attorney can send a *litigation hold* to the service provider, which will let the service provider know to preserve the content and metadata in the same fashion as a preservation letter. Your case will be easier if the bully does not have time to remove the content before the authorities see it. If the content is a naked picture of your child and your child is a minor, the legal stakes just got much higher for your suspect. However, if the bully obtained the photo from your child, the legal stakes just got higher for your child, as well.

In Chapter 2, we talked about social media sites and apps collecting information about you, your posting habits, devices, GEO coordinates, and so on. Now that information will actually come in handy. Not only can you get help from the social media site, but once it receives a legal letter from an attorney or the authorities, it can also give detailed information on exactly what account, device, operating system, IP address, and GEO coordinates the content was posted from, thereby helping to narrow down a suspect. Again, you might need a court order for this. Remember EXIF data? Even if the social media site strips out EXIF data from photos before they are posted, it still might have collected the original EXIF data from the photo. This will give identifying details about the camera that took the photo.

Terms of service

If you choose not to file charges but still want the content taken down, you can contact the service provider to get the account removed. Most social media sites such as Facebook will have strict terms of service that disallow users from posting harmful or negative content about other users. The service provider will most likely close the bully's account. The final option is to simply block the bully's social media so that you or your child can no longer see what is being posted. It is possible that if the bully sees that he or she cannot get to you or your child, he or she will move on.

The final and most important suggestion that I can give is to educate yourself and your children about bullying. Teach kids to understand what the signs are. Also, make sure that you keep an open dialogue with your child about bullying. Cyberbullying is, unfortunately, here to stay, but that does not mean you or your child have to put up with it!

8

Hoaxes, Spearfishing, and Fake Websites, Oh My!

> <((((o>

Scott Thomson had a very impressive resume. He had been a CEO at PayPal, and a senior executive at Inovant (a subsidiary of Visa) and at Barclay's Global Investors. He had been highly successful in his former positions and was considered a great catch for any company. In 2011 he won the Ernst & Young Entrepreneur of the Year Award for financial services for Northern California. He had gone to Stonehill College outside of Boston in the 1970s and had earned a degree in computer science, which led to his successful career.[1]

Manti Te'o, a Heisman Trophy–nominated football player at Notre Dame, had an amazing game against Michigan State, leading his team to beat the Spartans 20–3 in September 2012. He led his team to victory while under the heavy burden of double tragedy: his grandmother, and his girlfriend, Lennay Kekua, had both died within six hours of each other on September 11.[2]

Twenty-five-year-old half-Syrian, half-American Amina Abdallah Arraf al Omari, a lesbian known in Syria as a "Gay Girl in Damascus," caught the attention of the world in 2011. She was hailed as a hero for standing up against an oppressive Syrian opposition. Not only was Omari harassed frequently by Syrian secret police, but she touched the heart of the world by giving an honest portrayal of her life as a gay woman in a country in turmoil. She gave heartfelt interviews to the Western media and had a huge following of supporters. Then came the horrible news posted by Amina's cousin that she had been kidnapped.[3]

During the 2011 Republican primary race, GOP candidate Newt Gingrich amassed 1.3 million loyal Twitter followers. His opponent had only managed to get 63,000 followers. It would seem that based on these numbers, Gingrich was a much more significant contender because of his high social media popularity.[4]

All four of these stories are seemingly different. However, they all have one thing in common: The individuals involved used the Internet and social media to propagate untruths or hoaxes, and each of them got caught. Scott Thomson did indeed graduate from Stonehill; however he did not take a single computer science class there; rather, he had earned a degree in accounting. Manti Te'o's girlfriend, Lennay Kekua, was actually a 22-year-old man named Ronaiah Tuiasosopo. The "Gay Girl in Damascus" was a hoax perpetrated by Tom MacMaster, an American man studying in Scotland. Gawker and a social media search company called PeekYou conducted a detailed analysis on Newt Gingrich's Twitter followers and found that only 8 percent of them were real people; the rest were fake "bots" emulating legitimate users.

As of this writing most of us use social media in our daily lives. Unfortunately, a popular trend has taken hold in online culture: people misrepresenting themselves or outright lying, which has given birth to a host of hoaxes and scandals on the Internet. There seems to be a false sense of separation between real life and life online. This includes lying on a dating profile about your weight, height, or age, even though you know that you are eventually going to be found out when you meet the person in real life. So why do people think that they can get away with lying or stretching the truth online?

People often feel that they are protected or at least anonymous on the Internet because of privacy settings on social media sites. Because of this they may feel that they can control who has access to their data. This is augmented by the feeling of being hidden behind a screen—because they are protected and anonymous they can be whoever they want to be, better (or worse) versions of themselves. However, as we have learned in previous chapters, this is not reality. Yes, you can take certain steps to make yourself anonymous on the Internet, but because real life and online life have merged, it has become much harder to lie and get away with it. People have always lied or stretched the truth, but when you use the Internet or social media to do it, you have a much higher likelihood of getting caught, as we have already learned.

We have easy access to massive amounts of data on the Internet within seconds. By using modified statement analysis and the Catching the Catfisher Checklist, it is much easier to vet a person or determine if someone is not being truthful. Because there is a real person behind each online identity (which should have a normal pattern), you can much more easily determine when someone is not real, whether he or she simply has a Twitter account or multiple social media sites.

Lying on a resume is a big no-no. Dating back many years in online and paper sources (including his bio on Yahoo's Website), it was written that Scott Thomson had degrees in accounting and computer science from Stonehill College. You can't just lie in a published bio or online resume because real life merges with your online identity. Other people went to school with Thomson. Other people have worked with Thomson. And those other people know the truth. It would be very easy to use an online aggregator or portal like class-mates.com to find other people that Thomson went to school with who know the truth, unless he was able to get every single one of those people to lie for him.

There is debate as to whether or not Manti Te'o knew that his online girlfriend, Lennay Kekua, was fake or if he was duped. There is no debate as to whether or not Tom MacMaster knew that he was creating a fake identity with "A Gay Girl in Damascus." When someone is faking an on-line persona, there will always be red flags. If we were us-ing our Catching the Catfisher Checklist, and did an image search, we would have seen that in both the T'eo and Mac-Master cases they were stealing photos from someone else's Website.

Fake Twitter accounts are fairly easy to detect. Again, a fake Twitter account will most likely not have another pres-ence on the Internet, like a Facebook or LinkedIn account. Most importantly, a fake Twitter account will most likely not have other followers and will probably never be posted to. Also, a red flag would have been if one day Gingrich had 60,000 Twitter followers and the next day he had 1.3 million.

These hoaxes may be interesting and titillating, but they probably don't apply to you personally. Now let's talk about some prevalent hoaxes that might hit a bit closer to home.

Fake Reviews and the Dark Side of Reputation Cleaners

We have already established how important your online reputation is. Businesses can live or die based on their online reputations and the reviews they receive on sites such as Yelp, Citysearch, Google, and Yahoo. The reviews help consumers determine whether a service is safe and/or reliable. If you are planning to get laser hair removal or teeth whitening done, bad reviews could protect you from choosing a sketchy or outright inept provider. Likewise, if you need to charter a bus for your child's party, you probably want to make sure that the charter company is safe and has never had accidents or any other safety issues or violations. If you read online reviews of a particular bus company on Citysearch, Google, Yahoo, and Yelp, and they are all glowing and positive, you can probably assume that it's safe to use the company. But what if the reviews that you are relying on are fake?

In a recent sting operation, the New York Attorney General set up a fake yogurt shop that had received many bad reviews in order to target reputation-cleaner services or other services that create fake reviews:

> Eric Schneiderman announced agreements with 19 firms Monday that commissioned fake reviews and several reputation-enhancement companies that helped place reviews on sites like Citysearch, Google, Yahoo, and Yelp. They were fined a total of $350,000.

As part of a year-long investigation, dubbed Operation Clean Turf, officials posed as the owners of a Brooklyn yoghurt shop that had garnered negative reviews online. Fake reviews, written in Bangladesh, the Philippines, and Eastern Europe, were commissioned from reputation-management firms for as little as a dollar apiece. The investigation found reputation companies even wrote fake reviews of their own businesses denying that they wrote fake reviews.

The investigation found that SEO companies were using advanced IP spoofing techniques to hide their identities, and had set up hundreds of bogus online profiles on consumer review websites to post the reviews. Companies advertised for fake reviewers on listing site Craigslist and Freelance.com. One SEO firm required fake reviewers to have set up a Yelp account that was at least three months old and to have written at least 15 reviews before they were commissioned to write fake posts.[5]

So how can you protect yourself from employing services that are using fake reviews? The first thing to remember is that not everything that you read on the Internet is true! Along with remembering modified statement analysis (which we will cover in a later chapter), the following tips will help you vet a fake review:

- If you are reading reviews on Yelp or another service and you find that one day the company suddenly received a more than average number of reviews, you might be dealing with fake reviews.

- If you are reading positive reviews and the reviewers have not reviewed any other services, you might be dealing with a fake. Most reviewers will review many services and not just one.

- If the reviewer's profile only gives glowing reviews and gives 5 stars to everything, the reviewer could be fake.

- If the reviewer reviews companies and services in various locations that don't make sense, it could be a fake review. If a company is paid to create fake profiles and reviews, it will most likely reuse accounts. For example, if a reviewer that positively reviews a teeth-whitening company in New Jersey and then, within hours, positively reviews a bus service in San Francisco, the chances of a real person being able to be in two places at once is slim to none. If you see this, you can assume that the review is fake.

- Most sites such as Yelp have a way of contacting the reviewer. If you are suspicious, contact the reviewer and ask questions.

- Research the company on the Better Business Bureau's Website.[6] Almost all companies and services have a rating with the BBB. Because the BBB doesn't rate companies based on reviews and actively investigates complaints, it is more difficult to fake a good rating.

- Finally, most reviewers will be fairly specific and detailed about a service or company. A fake review will not be as detailed because the "reviewer" didn't actually use the service. The following examples show this.

Example 1:

This bus service is GREAT! Not only did the driver John bring water, which we forgot, but he also knew to take the Beltway when he saw that 66 was full of traffic, saving us at least an hour. John also knew all about the sites and even taught me (a history teacher) things about Washington D.C. history that I didn't know. I highly recommend this service.

Example 2:

This service is great! To be completely honest, I would highly recommend it. I had the best time and learned a lot on this tour. You should definitely use this service.

Notice how Example 1 is very detailed and specific. The reviewer knows details that indicate that she was indeed on the bus. In Example 2, the reviewer uses a qualifying statement (we'll learn about these later in the book)—"to be completely honest"—and there is a lack of personal detail. They don't give any details to back up their claim. Of course, not every generic review is a fake, but use your modified statement analysis and the tips listed previously to vet reviews and determine if a company is going to safe and reliable instead of just relying on a 5-star rating that may or may not be real.

Spear Phishing and Fake Websites

Most of us at some point have received an e-mail asking us to send money to help a starving child. They are pretty easy to recognize as hoaxes because the grammar is usually off and the story is usually ridiculous. But what about e-mails or hacked sites on the Internet where we are asked for personal information such as passwords, social security numbers, or account numbers? How can we learn to recognize when we are being conned into giving away details about ourselves or our company?

Spear phishing is much more clever and insidious than the random, obviously fake Nigerian e-mail scam that comes from someone we don't know. Spear fishing is an e-mail attempt that appears to come from someone you know and trust seeking access to your personal or your company's information. Often the e-mail will ask you to download something. The e-mail almost always looks legitimate. But if you follow the directions, you are actually downloading something to your computer that will give the spear phisher access to your machine or personal information. Yikes! Is what you are downloading really putting a piece of malicious code on your computer? Most legitimate companies have a security policy, which I recommend you become familiar with. But what if you were at work and you received the following e-mail?

> *From: IT_Department@Company.com*
> *To: Undisclosed*
>
> *Due to an emergency flaw in our company's software, please install the patch attached to this email. It is urgent that you do this immediately.*

First, I have never heard of an IT department that will send you a patch and ask you to install it yourself. Most IT departments have an Enterprise solution that updates patches automatically; or, the IT department will install the patch themselves. If you receive an e-mail like this, *do not* open it or download the patch. Almost all companies will have a computer security policy. Follow your company's security guidelines on what to do with the e-mail. They may ask that you alert your IT or security department and forward them the e-mail. Regardless, do not install the patch.

Sometimes spear phishers will not actually ask you download anything or reply with personal information. Instead, they will send you a link to a Website that looks identical to a legitimate site. If you are foolish enough to follow the link to the site, you will be asked to enter your personal details. Here is an example:

> *From: Security@Bank.com*
> *To: John Smith*
> *Mr. Smith:*
>
> *Due to hackers, we lost vital information about your account. Please follow the link below and re-enter your information.*
>
> *http://bank@banksecure.com*

When you go to the site, it looks legitimate. It *looks* real, and the e-mail itself came from a legitimate sounding e-mail address. Should you enter your details? The answer is no. No bank will ever ask you to go to a Website and enter your personal information. No bank or service will ever ask you in an e-mail to provide your user account, your password, or any personal information. If you receive this type of e-mail, delete it immediately and, if you want to take the time, report it to your bank. Never give out passwords or your account information to anyone, ever.

The Internet and social media connect us and give us instant access to information about people in ways we never could have imagined before, and there's no going back. Many of us converse with and follow people on social media whom we may have never met in person. It is crucial to protect yourself by vetting the people you interact with online, to determine if you are being conned or the victim of a hoax. Be careful to read between the fine lines and use the techniques that you've learned in this book to gauge whether or not a review, a news story, or an e-mail asking for your information is real. There could be more than just your reputation at stake.

<*(((><

9

Reading Deception Online

}-(((*>

There is a science dedicated to reading deception by learning to read body language. It is said that 90 percent of communication is nonverbal, meaning, of course, communication through body language and facial expressions. However, when reading deception in the online domain, you obviously don't have the ability to read anyone's body language unless you are using a video IP program such as Skype or Facetime. So, when reading deception in the online domain, we have to rely on the other 10 percent of communication, the written and spoken word. The way that you speak or write tells a lot about you. The words you choose and how you use them can tell other people if you are detailed or dramatic; often, they can tell whether you are in agreement with them or even whether you are being deceptive. This chapter will discuss how to weed out deception by using a modified law enforcement technique called *statement analysis*. We will also reverse the process and show you how and what to write to get what you want in a professional environment.

Modified Statement Analysis

Law enforcement officers are trained in statement analysis. According to Mark McClish in his book _10 Easy Ways to Spot a Liar_, "statement analysis is the process of analyzing a person's words to see if the person is being truthful or deceptive."[1] Everyone has an original and unique pattern of speaking and writing. This includes tone, inflection, and, most importantly for our purposes, choice and placement of words. There are many good books and YouTube tutorials on techniques that can be used to "baseline" a person's body language. When _baselining_ body language, we are looking for patterns to learn what is normal for that person so that when something changes, we know to look more closely at what triggered the change. The same techniques used in baselining can be applied to the way someone speaks or writes. The difference is that when baselining and building rapport with someone, instead of watching his body language, we are listening to the way he speaks or reading the words that he has written. We can get a sense of his vocabulary, word placement, and whether or not he uses a lot of detail (or tends to be vague in his descriptions and answers). Once we have baselined someone's unique pattern or signature, we can then assess what is normal for that person. When anomalies pop up, we know that something has made this person uncomfortable, potentially indicating deception. Most of what we will discuss in this chapter uses examples of speech, but the same deception techniques also apply to the written word, as we will see in these last two chapters.

A detective with whom I have kept in touch from my days as a digital forensic examiner left the public sector and took his skills to the commercial world, becoming a corporate security investigator. He told me about a case at a large commercial company. In the course of the company's daily business dealings, it had become apparent through some accounting irregularities that someone had been stealing from the company internally. Obviously the company wanted to find out quickly who the culprit was. Unfortunately most people in the company had access to the company's money. This company employed hundreds of people, so it would have taken forever to interview everyone. The former detective said that a typical trick used in this situation is to conduct a corporate survey. Instead of interviews, they would hand out a survey to all employees. In the survey, they would ask each person who they thought the culprit was, as well as some other typical, expected questions. The only question that mattered to the security team, however, was the question of what punishment ought to be given to the suspected thief when caught. Most people would respond to that question with harsh punishments such as imprisonment and financial repercussions. But anyone who responded with a lenient punishment or an excuse as to why the suspect might have done what he or she did was considered a suspect and brought in for questioning. This way they could narrow down the suspect pool and figure out who the true culprit was by conducting only a small number of interviews. The thinking was that whoever had done the crime didn't think that he or she deserved a harsh punishment and that this would come out in his or her answer to that question. As it turns out, it did, and in this particular case they eventually got a confession.

In my experience, people *want* to tell the truth. Most people are uncomfortable with lying and thus will typically give away clues that they are being dishonest. When reading body language for indications of deception, you are looking for this discomfort. Just as people who are uncomfortable will often cross their arms or stand behind a desk (to put distance between themselves and the cause of the discomfort), people will also do this in a figurative sense, with words, if they are uncomfortable with what they are saying *or* if they are being deceptive. The truth has a way of leaking out eventually. The same holds true with words as it does with body language. Just as body language gestures are often subconscious, the words that people choose to use and the placement of those words are also subconscious. In the next few pages we'll go over techniques that a liar might employ with his words and explain how you can learn to recognize them to become more aware of when someone might be lying to you.

Become a Human Lie Detector

Distancing or noncommittal technique

The distancing or noncommittal technique is commonly used when someone is extremely uncomfortable with what he is saying, most likely because he is lying. Subconsciously this person is simply unable to "put himself in" the story, so often he will avoid using committed or definitive words. Here's an example:

Officer: Did you take the car?
Suspect: *I was with Joe when it went down. Someone took the car.*

Notice the distance that the suspect is putting between himself and the theft of the car. He most likely was indeed with Joe. He acknowledges that the car was stolen but does not say whether or not he or Joe stole it. He distances himself from the situation by saying "someone" took the car instead of who. When he says that "[he] was with Joe," he is putting himself in the statement, indicating that this part of his statement is probably true. But notice he does not use "I" or "me" in relation to the car. Clearly, he does not want to put himself in that part of the story. Most people do not want to lie and want to leave themselves an "out." By saying "someone" instead of naming names, he is not entirely lying as far as he is concerned. Someone did indeed take the car and he probably knows who—he just isn't going to say. However, he is lying to the officer by distancing himself from the situation.

If he had not taken the car, the statement might have read more like this:

Officer: Did you take the car?
Suspect: *I saw it go down, but I did not take the car.*

In the second statement, the suspect definitively states that though he was present when the crime was committed, he did not perpetrate the crime. There is no distancing going on between him and the action, and he clearly puts himself in the statement about the car by using the word "I."

Another example of this technique is when the person uses noncommittal words:

Person 1: Do you want to go out again this weekend?
Person 2: *We should do this again sometime.*

Person 2 did not commit to the question either way. He did not say yes or no but instead said we "should" do this "sometime." Most likely this indicates that he probably doesn't want to go out again that weekend but he might want to keep Person 1 around as an option. Regardless of intent, those are very noncommittal words.

Depersonalization technique

A detective I have worked with who had 30 years of experience on the job once told me, "People want to think of themselves as good, trustworthy people and want others to view them as such." If someone knows he has done something wrong and he doesn't want you to know it or, even more importantly, doesn't want to acknowledge it even to himself, there is a tendency to depersonalize a situation. He doesn't want to be confronted with the truth that maybe he isn't such a good, trustworthy person after all. Using words to distance one's self from an action or person is a defensive and protective measure very similar to crossing your arms over your torso. Depersonalizing a situation resembles the distancing technique in that it is a way of minimizing a person's agency or role as an actor in an event. For violent criminals, depersonalizing is often their way of saying that the victim wasn't a real person.

"I'm going to say this again: I did not have sexual relations with that woman, Miss Lewinsky." This is a famous quote from former President Clinton when asked if he had had sex with Monica Lewinksy. By referring to her as "that woman" and then adding her formal last name almost as an afterthought, he was depersonalizing her and distancing himself from the actual person as well as the activity.

"Never answer the question"—aka the distraction technique

Another indication of deception is when someone talks around an issue but never actually answers the question directly. Sometimes the liar will also try to distract the questioner by attempting to change the subject entirely. Remember, none of these deception techniques is being done consciously. People typically do not know that they are using these techniques and therefore revealing some pretty telling clues that they are being deceptive. It is a way of protecting themselves—and perhaps you—from the truth. In some situations this technique is not necessarily done out of malice or the desire to lie, but because the other person doesn't want to hurt your feelings. Regardless, when this technique is used, the person is always uncomfortable or nervous with the question or situation:

Kay: Does this dress make me look fat?

Bob: *You look so much better in that blue one, and it really is better for the occasion.*

Notice that Bob never answers the question. He is uncomfortable with the question and probably doesn't want to hurt Kay's feelings. So instead of telling the truth, Bob distracts Kay with a suggestion. Notice that Bob never puts himself in the answer. He does not say, "I think that you look better in this other dress" or "I think that this one would be better for the occasion," which means he is also using the distancing technique. You can tell a lot by this answer. I hate to say it, but if you are asking this question and get this response, the bad news is that the other person probably thinks that the dress makes you look fat. The good news, though, is that you have a really good friend who cares enough about you that he doesn't want you to look bad and also doesn't want to hurt your feelings—a tough line for anyone to walk!

A more malicious example of the distraction or "not answering the question" technique is illustrated in the following two examples:

Employee: Will you help me get this promotion by giving me a good recommendation?

Boss: *This sounds like such a great opportunity for you. You would definitely do a great job in that position.*

If you were not paying careful attention to the words, you might read this response as positive and assume that the boss meant that, yes, she will support the promotion and write a good recommendation. But upon further examination, this is not the case. The boss has distanced herself from the situation by not putting herself in the answer—again, note the lack of "I" or "me" here. She talks *around* the real issue in order to distract her employee from her true feelings. Bottom line: She doesn't answer the question. This is a very good indication that this boss either needs some time to think about it or doesn't want the employee to be promoted to that position. Regardless of the reason, she may very well not support the promotion.

The second malicious example of the distraction technique is as follows:

Wife: I've noticed that a lot of days, you say you're working late, but when I call your office, they say that you're not there but that you're with Glenda. Are you cheating on me with Glenda?

Husband: *Dammit, I work so hard to put food on this table and you don't even appreciate it!*

Notice that the husband does indeed put himself in the answer, but not only does he not answer the question; he makes the problem about his wife. This is "distraction by blameshifting." Notice that the husband brings up another issue entirely, which is intended to make his wife feel guilty and at fault so that she forgets what the question was. This is a guy who feels self-righteous and guilty at the same time, and who feels that his needs far outweigh those of his wife. There is no mutual respect in this relationship, at least not right now.

The "too much or not enough detail" technique

Have you ever known someone who speaks in great detail about everything? This person can remember things that are very specific to an event. She probably likes to use as many words as possible. If this type of person suddenly becomes vague in her descriptions, or suddenly clams up or starts getting parsimonious with her words, you know that something is making her uncomfortable. This can be an indication of deception. When people lie, they are using a different part of their brain to create the lie than the one they use when reciting from memory an event that really happened. A federal agent friend of mine told me a story in which a suspect in a money laundering case used very descriptive language and was able to accurately remember things like his locker number from high school. He talked a lot, but when he was asked a question that made him uncomfortable (about where he was the day of the crime), he was suddenly vague with his words and unable to remember events that had taken place a week before. It turned out that he was lying and he eventually confessed.

Conversely, if a person that you have baselined as taciturn or reticent suddenly begins to use tons of adverbs, he is likely uncomfortable and buying time to think up an answer. If people are not telling you the truth and the stakes are high, they tend to become nervous. Some people actually freeze up. If someone who usually is either a detailed speaker or a normal speaker suddenly takes long pauses, drags out his words, or uses vague words or descriptions, again, he is buying time. He is trying to come up with the right words to say or a lie that he thinks will satisfy the questioner.

On the other hand, some people who are trying to concoct a falsehood begin to talk a lot and give almost ridiculously detailed accounts. Such people are also trying to buy time. Most people do not give overly detailed accounts of their lives or events. They put themselves in their stories but give only enough detail to show that they are coming from memory and not fiction. Sometimes a story will be partially true, and if you are listening to or reading an account carefully, you will notice a difference in speech pattern, which will enable you to gauge where the truth ends and the falsity begins. Look at the following two examples and try and discern who is lying:

Example 1

Officer: Did you see the car get stolen?

Respondent: *No, I was at home watching TV and I heard some commotion outside. By the time I got to the window, the car was gone.*

Example 2

Officer: Did you see the car get stolen?

Respondent: *Well let's see. That was on Thursday, so I must have been watching my favorite TV show,* Project Runway. *I really adore that show. It's so good. Have you ever seen it? Yeah, I love it. I think that it was the episode where they made dresses out of nontraditional materials like candy or stuff from a hardware store, so, yeah, I don't really know anything about the car because I was busy watching TV.*

If you chose the second example as the lie, you are correct. There is so much wrong with the second respondent's statement. In the first example, the respondent provides sufficient details to show that he was home watching TV and heard something but did not witness the event. In the second example, the respondent is attempting to distract the officer and buy more time to spin his yarn. "Well, let's see" is a nonessential phrase that is often used it to take up time while the respondent thinks of what to say next. As well, the detail provided in the second example is far too involved to be completely true. Notice the use of the distancing or noncommittal technique by the use of the word "must" in the phrase "I must have been." If the person had been watching the show, he would not have used "must have been" or "I think it was the episode." Rather than using distancing or inconclusive words, he would have been much more definitive. He would have simply stated that he was watching the show. The use of the phrase "must have been" indicates that the respondent is not taking ownership of his part in the story and thus is not being totally truthful. He rambles on about the show and then states that he was too busy watching TV to have noticed anything. By providing such extraneous details of the episode, he is trying to get the officer to believe that there is no way that he could have remembered so much if he hadn't really been watching the show.

The "answering a question with a question" technique

Another deception technique involves stalling for time by answering a question with a question. After baselining some people, you will see that this is often just a bad habit. If you yourself use this technique sparingly, it can be a useful tool to help you gather your thoughts. Regardless of whether or not someone is being deceptive or just trying to gather her thoughts, this is a way for a respondent to buy more time to think of the best answer. When you are reading someone using this technique, you have to put the whole answer into context. If you are asking a complicated question and get the answer thrown back at you as a question, the respondent might just be trying to figure out the answer. If you continue to receive answers in the form of questions, there is a good chance that the person is trying to distract you and is being—surprise, surprise!—deceptive. In the first example that follows, the respondent is asked a tough question and demands time to think of the answer. There is no deception or maliciousness in this case:

Questioner: What is the quadratic formula?
Respondent: *What is the quadratic formula?* [The respondent makes a thinking gesture and then attempts to answer.]

In the next example, the respondent is trying to buy time to come up with an answer. Again, context is important here:

Questioner: The office door was not locked last night. Were you the last person to leave?

Respondent: *Uh, was I the last person to leave last night?*

If the respondent really knew that she had locked the door or was not the last person to leave, or if she really didn't know whether she was the last person to leave, she would have responded by saying something like this:

I was the last to leave, but I know I locked the door.
I was not the last person to leave. Chuck was working late.
I don't know if I was the last to leave. Can we ask around?

The "tense hopping" technique

Another deception technique involves changing tenses inappropriately. Keep in mind that some people are naturally lacking in grammar and syntax, and thus will change tenses frequently. But again, if you have baselined someone as an articulate speaker, and he suddenly starts tense-hopping, he might not be telling you the truth. We live in the present, tell stories from the past, and talk about what will happen in the future. When someone is narrating a story about something that already happened and keeps changing tenses, using past, present, and sometimes future, he is likely trying to piece together an account that is not entirely truthful. Here's an example:

Questioner: Did you tell Justin that I did not like his project?

Respondent: *Justin and I had coffee last week. He asked me what you **said** about his presentation. I **told** him that you **liked** it.*

In this example the respondent keeps his account of the story in the correct past tense and is therefore telling the truth. In the following example, notice how the respondent changes tenses:

Questioner: Did you tell Justin that I did not like his presentation?

Respondent: *Justin and I had coffee last week. He asked me what you said about his presentation. I **am telling** him that I really **like** it.*

Notice how the respondent tells a story from the past, and retains the part about her having had coffee last week and Justin asking the question in the past ("He asked me"). But the respondent suddenly jumps to telling this story (which already happened) using present descriptors ("I am telling" and "I really like"). It is likely true that the respondent went for coffee with Justin last week, and did indeed ask her what she thought of the presentation, but it is most likely not true that the respondent told Justin that she liked the presentation. The wonky verb tenses belie her story.

Remember that when someone is creating a false account of a story, his or her mind is trying to make up parts of the story on the fly. The respondent here knows she is not telling the truth. By couching things in the present tense, she is trying to re-create the story as she sees it unfolding in her mind's eye, in the present. Because historical events occur in linear order, the respondent is clearly making up a story in the present as she is telling her version of a past story. This can get confusing, which is why the present-tense words inevitably slip out.

The "word swapping" technique

Another deception technique involves changing an important or key word. Typically people use a vocabulary of words, a lexicon, that is normal for them. For example, if someone is talking about a gun, he will usually describe it *as* a gun. People are comfortable with their vocabulary and comfortable with the words they typically use for people, places, and things. If someone suddenly starts swapping typical language for other words that don't seem to fit, this can be an indication that he is not comfortable with something he's saying. An example:

Officer: Are you comfortable with guns? Do you own a gun?

Suspect: *I do not own a gun. I am not at all comfortable with guns.*

Obviously this is an exaggerated example, but notice how the suspect continues referring to a gun *as* a gun.

Officer: Did you see a gun?

Suspect: *I did not see a gun. There was definitely no firearm anywhere nearby.*

Notice that the suspect who had been baselined to use the word "gun" suddenly changes his terminology and refers to the gun as a firearm. This is an indication that this suspect is not telling the truth—either about there being a gun involved in the crime, or his involvement in that crime, or both.

The "qualifier" technique

A liar will use qualifying statements to prove to others that she is being truthful. Usually, if you listen to the qualifying statement, you will find that the opposite is true. Unfortunately, I have noticed that it is common these days for people to use qualifying statements even when they are being truthful. By using them, stories take on a more dramatic quality, making for a better, more exciting story. In fact, I find myself using qualifiers all the time for the same reason. So make sure that you baseline a person before you assume that he or she is lying if you hear qualifiers.

Here are a few examples of qualifiers:

- "Don't panic."

- "There is nothing to worry about, but...."

- "To be completely honest with you...."

- "I am being totally truthful with you."

These phrases can reveal that someone is trying a bit too hard to convince. For example, if someone says, "Look, I didn't want to tell you this, but..." you can rest assured that this person very much wanted to tell you whatever it is he or she is about to say! All the detectives I interviewed about qualifiers stated that in their experience, when a suspect uses qualifiers, it almost always means that the person is not telling the truth.

Being too general

This is similar to but slightly different than the non-committal technique. You can spot this technique when someone is being (uncharacteristically) too general. This is a very important technique to understand because we will refer to it frequently in the next few chapters. In the following example a friend has lied to another friend, claiming that she was sick, to get out of attending a birthday party. I wouldn't characterize this as a malicious lie, but it is a lie nonetheless. In the last chapter, which shows real examples of this technique, we will see that it can actually be very dangerous.

Friend throwing the party: I am so sorry that you got sick. What did you have?

Lying friend: *Oh, you know, just a cold. No big deal. How was the party?*

Notice how the lying friend is very general in her description. Also notice the immediate use of the distraction technique by asking how the party was. If this is the type of friend who usually gives great detail on everything and she gives you this answer, she is most likely being deceptive. However, if your friend is the type who doesn't like to talk about herself and tends to be more private, this is just her being herself. This is why baselining is so important, especially with this particular deceptive technique.

The following chart is a quick refresher on all these techniques. Keep this page marked because we will be using it in the final chapter.

Quick Refresher Chart to Use When Reading Deception

Distancing Technique or Noncommital Words	Distancing self from story by not putting himself in story. Using inconclusive words.
Depersonalizing Technique	Not using subject's name or referring to him/her using very general words.
Never Answer the Question or Distraction Technique	Talking around the issue but never really answering the question.

Too Much or Not Enough Detail Technique	Using far too many words (could be to bide time to think up answer). Very vague, using as few words as possible.
Answering a Question With a Question Technique	Biding for time by answering a question with a question.
Tense-Hopping Technique	Changing verb tenses inappropriately for the context.
Word Swapping Technique	Using words that are out of character.
Qualifier Technique	Using statements such as "to be honest."
Too General Technique	Not giving specific details.

}-(((*> **10**

Catching the Catfishers

> <((((o>

In Chapter 9, we discussed statement analysis techniques frequently used to determine deception through the written and spoken word. By baselining someone's speech patterns and written words, we can establish if someone is being deceptive. Just as it is in the physical world, it is important to protect your online identity by being able to read deception in online profiles so that you can adapt your responses and protect yourself and your children. Now we are going to take the techniques learned in Chapter 9, enhance them, and apply them to reading deception in social media.

Early on I mentioned that many commercial companies use data analytic software that can determine whether someone is who they say they are. At a very basic level, the software counts each time certain words are used and in what context, memorizing typical word placement, grammar, spelling, and so on to form a database that essentially comprises a powerful baseline or normal pattern for this particular identity. For our purposes, this is something that we can do without expensive software.

As we learned in prior chapters, we are looking for anomalies in a baselined pattern to determine potential deception. If you ask a question via e-mail or social media and do not get an answer, or if the respondent uses one of the techniques we learned earlier (such as distracting, talking around the question, or blatantly ignoring it and bringing up a new topic), that person clearly does not want to answer your question.

The Power of the Online Relationship

The relationships built through online chat and social media are just as powerful and real as relationships built in the "real world." With the invention of online dating and social media, very strong relationships can be formed in which both participants fall very much in love with each other, even though they may have never actually met in person. Sometimes people who meet this way and get to know each other through these media claim to have been able to get closer than they would have if they had initially met in person. I know some of us might find it unusual to get to know someone using these media, but your kids probably understand it perfectly. They all connect using social media! It is normal for them to deepen their friendships and other personal relationships in the online domain. Connecting on social media is as important to their generation as using the telephone was to others—if not more so, because they have a constant and on-demand connection to all of their friends at all times. I met my husband in 2002 in New York City. Matt lived in New

York and I lived in California and was traveling to New York for work. I really liked him and wanted to get to know him better, but there were about 3,000 miles in the way. However, we began an online relationship using Instant Messenger. Our connection was very real, and I felt that we got to know each other in greater detail because we were using this medium for communication. I have made connections with many experts in my field and have gotten to know them pretty well, even though we have never met in person. We are lucky that we have this ability to connect and reach out to people whom we would never have been able to connect with prior to the invention of social media. But with all that connectivity and convenience there comes a price and some caveats.

How to Vet People Online: Catching the Catfisher

Society and popular culture have established that Internet-based online dating sites and social media are very real ways to get to know someone and establish professional or personal relationships, but you have to take some precautions. The news is filled with stories of people getting to know someone online and ending up victims of fraud or having been deceived in other ways. MTV airs a program called *Catfish*[1] in which two guys interview people in online relationships who haven't physically met and find ways to introduce them in person. In almost every episode, it comes to light that one of the people in the relationship is not who he or she claims to be, or is at least being deceptive in some other significant way. The creator of the show, Nev Schulman, created the term "catfish" after speaking with his online love interest's husband, Vince Pierce, who happens to be a fisherman. Vince said:

They used to tank cod from Alaska all the way to China. They'd keep them in vats in the ship. By the time the codfish reached China, the flesh was mush and tasteless. So this guy came up with the idea that if you put these cods in these big vats, put some catfish in with them and the catfish will keep the cod agile. And there are those people who are catfish in life. And they keep you on your toes. They keep you guessing, they keep you thinking, they keep you fresh. And I thank god for the catfish because we would be droll, boring and dull if we didn't have somebody nipping at our fin.[2]

How can you protect yourself and your children from being deceived or conned in this manner? How can you learn how to adapt your reactions? How can you ensure that the people with whom you or your children are communicating are actually who they claim to be? It is getting harder these days for deceptive people to pretend to be someone they're not not with the advent of video technologies such as Skype, but it is still very possible to be deceived. This is why you need to know how to piece together the digital puzzle pieces an online identity leaves behind to look at the whole picture and get a sense of who someone really is. By the end of this chapter, you will have a checklist of things to look for that will indicate whether someone is who they say they are. By using this checklist, you will have the tools you need to catch the catfisher!

The Red Flags

Red Flag One: Won't Skype

If the person you've met online doesn't want to have telephone contact or is unwilling to video chat by using a program such as Skype, he is probably hiding something. This is your first clue that something might be off. He might claim that his camera isn't working or that he can't afford a camera, but let's face it: Most smartphones, tablets, and laptops dating back to 2008 have onboard cameras. I don't care what he tells you—there is no legitimate reason why a person couldn't Skype with you.

Red Flag Two: Digital Puzzle Pieces and the Generation Gap

As of this writing, almost everyone in America has a "presence" on the Internet. As we have discussed, people leave trails of digital puzzle pieces behind with every posted content. We have to keep in mind that the average number of digital puzzle pieces or breadcrumbs that you will find on someone who you are trying to vet can be determined generationally. Obviously this is not true for all cases, but typically Baby Boomers will not have as many digital breadcrumbs to follow as someone who grew up in the Millennial Generation. Likewise, the Millennial generation will not have as many breadcrumbs to follow as those who were born with the Internet, the so-called Generation Z kids. According to an About.com article, "Names of Generations" by Matt Rosenberg, the generational breakdown is as follows:

- 2000/2001–Present—New "Silent Generation" or "Generation Z"
- 1980–2000—"Millennials" or "Generation Y"
- 1965–1979—"Generation X"
- 1946–1964—"Baby Boomers"

People born in the 2000s and up (Generation Z) will typically have Internet breadcrumbs that can be followed back to their birth because their parents began to create their digital identities by posting birth announcements, photographs, and information about them on social media sites. In fact, many Generation Z'ers will actually have a digital presence *before* their births. Mothers will typically post their "We are Pregnant" status on social media and continue to update as they move along during their pregnancies, leaving behind many digital puzzle pieces including the gender of the child ("It's a boy!!"). It is very rare to find someone from Generation Z in the United States whose parents have not created an online presence for him or her. If you (or your children) are talking and having an online relationship with someone who claims to be from Generation Z, just follow the digital breadcrumbs. If someone actually is from this generation, you will be able to find massive amounts of data about him or her, such as parental postings or other content such as baby pictures. If you do not find a normal amount of digital puzzle pieces throughout the Internet from or about a Gen Z'er, you might have caught a catfish. Remember, Generation Z'ers will post a lot of content, but will also have a lot of content posted about them by parents and others.

Lori Drew was a mother who created a fake Myspace page in order to bully and humiliate her neighbor Meagan Meier in 2006.[3] Drew created a profile claiming to be a 16-year-old male named Josh Evans. She messaged Meagan pretending to be this guy. Eventually they became involved in a relationship that was very real to Meagan until, one day, Josh Evans told her that he didn't want to be friends with her anymore. This story turned tragic when Meagan committed suicide.

If Josh Evans had been a real person, and if this happened in 2014 rather than in 2006, there would have been many digital puzzle pieces to follow that would have indicated that Josh Evans was not a real person. To understand what is not normal, we have to first establish a pattern of what *is* normal. So let's look at what would comprise normal digital breadcrumbs if Josh were a real 16-year-old kid born in Generation Z. Most Gen Z'ers are friends with their parents on Facebook, and vice versa. If the Gen Z'er that you are trying to vet is not, that could be a red flag. As well, the parents would most likely have chronological "temporal" puzzle pieces about their child on their social media site, meaning a history of postings about the child that follws a logical time line as he grew up, such as "Josh was born," "Josh is walking at 1," "Josh is going to preschool," etc. A real and normal Gen Z'er like Josh would have many friends on his Facebook profile. Josh would probably have a Twitter account that he updates frequently. Josh would make frequent references to his school and it would probably be easy to find him on the school's Website. He would have friends at school and be knowledgeable about teachers and daily school activities, and probably post about them. Josh might follow and post on blogs that were of interest to him. He would frequently post real-time photos of himself hanging out with friends or photos that chronologically detail his activities. He would have a pattern that is typical of most kids of that generation.

Now let's look at what would be anomalous. If a person who claims to have been born in the Generation Z era suddenly appears and has no other presence anywhere else on the Internet, a presence that follows a normal, temporal pattern or time line, has only one social media site that just seemed to appear one day with no (or just a few) friends who never post on his site, this is a good indication that this person might be a catfisher. We discussed that a normal Gen Z'er would have friends posting about his activities and comments related to those activities. If a person posts only one or very few photos and does not reference school or activities with friends, it is a good indication that he (or she) is not real. If he won't send you photos in real time on demand, that's another red flag. It would have been almost impossible for Lori Drew to keep up with a fake Twitter account, maintain regular postings, and create a fake online presence that a normal 16-year-old would have. Creating a fake Josh Evans that would be believable in 2014 would be much more difficult than it was in 2006.

But what if you are talking with someone who claims to be a member of an older generation and friending them could affect your professional reputation? In 2010, Thomas Ryan, the co-founder and managing partner of Cyber Operations and Threat Intelligence for Provide Security, decided to try an experiment to present at the DEF CON/Blackhat security conference. He created a fake online identity named Robin Sage and tried to make her realistic enough so that he could get senior executives and senior officials in the DoD and Intelligence communities to believe that she was real, friend her, and potentially give away information:

> "By joining networks, registering on mailing lists, and listing false credentials, the conditions were then met to research people's decisions to trust and share information with the false identity," according to the description of the session. Ryan deliberately chose an attractive young female's picture to prove that sex and appearance plays in trust and people's eagerness to connect with someone.

> By the end of the 28-day experiment, Robin finished the month having accumulated hundreds of connections through various social networking sites. Contacts included executives at government entities such as the NSA, DOD and Military Intelligence groups. Other friends came from Global 500 corporations. Throughout the experiment Robin was offered gifts, government and corporate jobs, and options to speak at a variety of security conferences, said Ryan.[4]

This project really hurt some professional careers. A lot of high-ranking government officials were ridiculed and had their judgment questioned. National security could have been in jeopardy.

We have already established that there will be fewer digital puzzle pieces to follow with a member of the Baby Boomer generation than with a member of Generation X, and even fewer than with a member of the Millennial generation. However, there will still be some breadcrumbs somewhere that will enable you to vet someone from this generation. Again, you want to look at what is normal. Most people, regardless of their generation, have an online presence. They might have a Facebook account. They might post on a blog. They might list their achievements, such as awards, white papers, or conferences that they've spoken at. They will most likely have a professional social media profile. If a Gen X'er's presence suddenly appears online with few friends, few photos, no real-time photos or other friends commenting on the site, and you can only find the person on one social media site, you might be dealing with a catfisher. Robin Sage had a LinkedIn account, but if you tried to research her, you wouldn't have been able to find any other digital puzzle pieces or realistic social media sites with content in which she had an online presence.

Geographic and Real-Time Photos

It is also important to look for discrepancies in stories. Are facts presented correctly? Geographic references must match. Are facts about their geography not true? Does their story match with what is going on in their geographic location? For example, does someone who claims to live in New Jersey during a huge snowstorm make proper references to the storm happening around them? Do they post or send you pictures of the storm as a "real" person would? Do they make references to known local entities, such as restaurants and bars? Do they know what the weather is if you were to ask them without having to take time to look it up?

Change in the Story

Watch for changes in the story. If you are trying to keep up a fake identity and a lie, it is hard to keep your story straight because you are continually referencing your real life as you create this fake identity. For example, if you are having an online relationship with a man claiming to be named Jake, but Jake is in fact a woman named Tina, little facts from Tina's life will pop out. If Jake claims to have no family but Tina has two sisters, Jake might accidently make reference to his sisters. You want to be aware of discrepancies in stories. If something doesn't feel right, it probably isn't.

Records Search

You also want to research phone numbers. There are many reverse searches that you can perform on the Internet (some free, some not) to find out whom a phone number is registered to. Sometimes a number is unlisted, but often it is. If a phone number is registered to a different name, you might be dealing with someone who is not who he or she claims to be. Spokeo can help you search for other online presences for a name. You can also perform pretty comprehensive background searches on a name and location to vet a person. Almost everyone is in a public database somewhere. If you can't find this person anywhere, you might be dealing with a catfisher. You can also research open public sites, depending on what this person has told you. For example, if John Doe, whom you have been speaking with online, claims to own a home in Arlington, Virginia, you can easily search public housing records to see if John Doe owns a house there. If you find nothing, John Doe might be lying to you about the house. Or, he might not be John Doe at all.

Photo Search

You can use Google Photo Search or another photo-matching program to see if photos of your online friend appear anywhere else on the Internet under someone else's online identity. If someone has snagged a photo from someone else's profile, you have a good shot of finding the other profile.

Follow Your Instinct

If you have a gut feeling that something is wrong and that the person you are communicating with might not be telling you the whole truth, you have to listen to that instinct and open your mind to the possibility that you may be right.

Protecting Yourself From Predators:

Lack of Detail

During my career as a digital forensic analyst, the most difficult major crimes cases that I worked were the exploitation of children cases. I have worked many of these cases, sadly. While analyzing the chats and online profiles of the suspected pedophiles, one personality trait stuck out for me. In most cases, the suspected pedophile would go to almost any length to try to deceive his target. Indeed, he would become obsessed with the target. For example, such a person might claim to be a 13- or 14-year-old boy from another school in another state, when he begins talking to his target. He might research the Website of the school he claims to attend and then pick a 13- or 14-year-old boy as his "cover" persona. Or he might just make up a fake persona. If a predator is claiming to be another person who actually exists, with a little research and by using the checklist in this chapter, you can determine this fairly quickly. If he is pretending to be a random 13-year-old boy named John Doe from a nearby school, chances are that the real John Doe will also have an online persona. By searching for the real John Doe and using your handy checklist, you can determine where the profiles clash and figure out which one is the *real* John Doe. The ill-intentioned adult most likely will have scoured the real John Doe's school Website for information about the school and learned a bit about the boy. If he has created a fake persona, the predator may even go so far as to "friend" some of other students from the school he claims to attend. However, understand that the other students will actually know if this person is the real boy they see every day. Some kids are friend collectors and thus may not care that they don't know him (and friend him anyway), but there will be a distinct lack of detail in their friend's posts, or very few outside comments to the fake profile. There will be a distinct lack of detail in his comments, if there are any at all.

It is important to teach your children how to use the checklist for their protection. When vetting a suspected catfisher or predator, it is important to pay very close attention to the small details that I have discussed here. A real 13- or 14-year-old child would talk about very specific details such as his teachers' names, his friends' names, where he likes to get lunch, what the food is like at the school, extracurricular activities he takes part in—again, all with a high level of detail. Someone who has malevolent, obsessive intentions toward your child is going to scour the Internet to try to make his fake online identity appear accurate and realistic. Notice the difference in the two following examples:

Example 1

Post: "Great game tonight. The team won. What are you doing?"

Notice the lack of detail, along with the deflection technique. Also notice that the person did not put him- or herself in the statement. There is no "I" or "we."

Example 2

Post: "You should have seen it. Wood threw the ball to Shep at the last second and he ran 20 yards for the touchdown. BTW it was FREEZING in the bleachers!!!"

Notice the level of detail used. The writer in Example 2 refers to the players by their names because he knows them. The players are probably also his Facebook friends. He knew that it was cold, and you can see that knowledge come through in his post. The writer's level of detail is very specific because he was actually there.

Ask Their Friends

If you suspect that the person you are communicating with is hiding something from you or being deceptive, and he has an online social media profile, there is nothing wrong with reaching out to *his* friends and asking them about your target. You can say that you are a friend of theirs. If the "friend" does not know the other person, that's a huge red flag. Also, feel free to do a little sleuthing on these so-called friends. If your friend has only a few friends, and those friends do not appear anywhere else on the Internet, those friends could be decoys made up by the ill-intentioned predator or catfisher.

When looking to vet a real person, keep your Catching the Catfisher Checklist handy.

Catching the Catfisher Checklist

- ☐ Do they refuse to have telephonic or Skype conversations?

- ☐ Do they have an appropriate and normal amount of online digital puzzle pieces for their generation?

- ☐ If they are Gen Y'ers or Gen Z'ers, are they friends with their parents on social media?

- ☐ If they are a Gen Z'er, do their parents have a time line of their child on their social media?

- ☐ Do they have many friends commenting and carrying on conversations?

- ☐ Do they have more than one social media outlet that they use at least a few times a day?

- ☐ Look at the fine details of their conversations. Are they knowledgeable, and do they give specifics about normal activities such as school or work?

- ☐ Do they follow any blogs and post to them?

- ☐ Do they post regular, new photos of themselves, or are they willing to send a real-time "just took this photo" to you?

- ☐ If a Gen Y'er or Gen Z'er, do they have a school association?

☐ If they are a professional, do they have a professional social media site listing achievements and have realistic endorsements from others?

☐ Do they make the correct geographical references and present facts correctly?

☐ Do they show up in public searches?

☐ Do their facts seem consistent?

☐ Is there another profile that is different in the same person's name?

☐ Do they come up with a different profile when you do a photo search?

☐ If you have reached out to their friends, do they seem real and like they know the person?

☐ Does something just seem off?

If you cannot appropriately answer these questions to your satisfaction, you are likely dealing with someone who is not who he claims to be. Perhaps you've caught the catfisher.

Deception in Dating: How to Read Deception in Dating Profiles

People lie on dating sites more often than you would think. Sometimes the lies are relatively insignificant, like adding a few inches to one's height, or a few less pounds to one's weight. But sometimes these lies are much more insidious and harmful. Think of the person claiming to be looking for a serious relationship who really wants a fling. For someone who is really putting herself out there in search of Mr. Right, this could be disastrous. So how can you tell if someone is not being honest in a dating profile?

Vetting Photos

You can learn a lot from photographs that people send you or choose to use in their dating profiles. In my experience and training as a digital forensic examiner who supports law enforcement, blurred photos often indicate that a person is hiding something. Always be wary of online profiles where you cannot see the person's full face or eyes in a photo. Maybe they are wearing a hat in every photo that covers part of their face. Maybe all their photos are in profile. Maybe they are all slightly blurry. They may be hiding something that wouldn't be a big deal to you (such as thinning hair), but it might also be something much more significant.

More Word Games

How someone presents him- or herself with words can give you a lot of clues as to whether they are on the up and up. You should look at every word that a person chooses to use in his profile carefully. If a person uses the word "I" and never uses the word "we" or "you" when talking about what he is looking for, the guy might be self-centered. Look for extreme adjectives such as "adore" or "despise" or words such as "very" or "really." These words are not just for show; they are indicators of strong feelings. If someone keeps repeating a phrase or saying the same thing in different ways, what he is saying is very important and probably a high priority. Remember, the truth always finds a way of leaking out.

Now that we are armed with modified statement analysis techniques, we can easily determine who is being truthful and who isn't. The following profiles are from a free dating Website. They are all from men. I have slightly modified them to protect identities. Each man claims in his profile that he is searching for a long-term, committed relationship. But as we'll see, this may not be completely true!

Profile 1:

I despise routine, so I like to try new things and meet new people daily. Recently I realized I was taking the Washington D.C. area for granted and have decided to go exploring and meet new people. So I'm here to find a partner in crime to join me. It will be no easy task. Sometimes we'd do cool things like explore the underground tunnels at the National Cathedral or meet Senators at posh networking events. Other times we'd go to the Postal Museum or remove syringes from Heritage Park. I'm looking for someone who can make all of these things enjoyable for me. Are you up to the challenge?

I just look for four things in a potential date: 1) She gets excited about the small things; 2) She's confident and independent and she's fine on her own; 3) She's witty and clever and not super clingy or waiting by the phone 4) She's girl next door pretty and not runway beautiful.

On first glance, he looks like a great catch. However, let's look at some key phrases:

- despise routine

- potential date

- meet new people daily, exploring, meet new people

- I'm looking for someone who can make all of these things enjoyable for me

- independent and she's fine on her own and not super clingy or waiting by the phone

The man in his profile writes that he "despises routine." "Despise" is a strong word, indicating intense feelings (in this case, hatred) about something. Relationships are all about routine. For someone to indicate that he not only doesn't like routine, but "despisess" it says that this could be someone who is not yet ready to settle down. He mentions that he wants to meet new people twice. In the first sentence, he wants to meet new people "daily." His words indicate that he wants to meet a lot of people, perhaps as friends, perhaps as romantic partners; but either way, his words show that he has prioritized meeting new people as something that is really important to him. Subconsciously he is showing that he probably does not want settle down with just one person. He states, "I'm looking for someone who can make all of these things enjoyable for me." Look carefully at the words. He wants someone to make things fun for him. His words tell you that his needs will take priority over yours, and it is up to the other person to entertain him. Based on this statement alone, this is not a person who will compromise easily. What he says, goes. The phrase "potential date" is as glaring an example of the non-committal deception technique as you can get. It indicates that this person is looking for a casual encounter. The two statements "independent and she's fine on her own" and "not super clingy or waiting by the phone" further reinforces the idea that this guy is looking for something casual. He wants someone who also is looking for a fling. No one wants someone who is clingy and especially not super clingy. By choosing to state this, he is indicating that he's had issues with this in the past with other women. By using the words "super clingy" and "not waiting by the phone" together, he is indicating that perhaps in the past he dated someone who was more into the relationship than he was. He probably just stopped calling and perhaps the girl didn't get the message that he wasn't interested. Regardless, this is probably not the most mature fish in the sea.

Based on the words he is using, he is looking for a friend or a fling. Even though he claims to be looking for a serious, long-term relationship, when you put the pieces together, this person is just looking to casually date and does not want to take things too fast or too seriously. He is not ready to settle down and just wants to play. He wants to date many girls, have some fun and meet many new people (by people, of course, he means women). If a woman were to answer his ad and date him, I would tell her that this is the kind of guy she would have good time with but not to expect anything serious. And don't be surprised if he suddenly stops calling. As he said, don't wait by the phone!

Profile 2:

I should emphasize that if you are very, very smart, and/ or knowledgeable about subjects where I'm not, and eager to share, these are good things. I understand there are a lot of ridiculous, insecure man-children who get threatened by smart women, but this is one fault from which I do not suffer. Go ahead and knock my socks off.

I believe the foundation of a romantic connection is a great friendship. That said, I'm long past the point where I bother with "just friends;" I'm lucky enough to enjoy many close, deep friendships in my life already, so if you know if it's not gonna happen between us, let's not waste each other's time.

With this in mind, message me if you are ready to meet the one.

Let's look closely at some key phrases:

- eager to share

- I understand there are a lot of ridiculous insecure man-children who get threatened by smart women

- foundation of a romantic connection is a great friendship. That said, I'm long past the point where I bother with "just friends"

- not waste each other's time

- ready to meet the one

He uses present and future tense words, indicating that he is looking for a partner to be with him now and in the future. He has thought a lot about what makes a good "foundation for a romantic connection," indicating that he is ready to lay that foundation with someone. The phrases "long past the point" and "not waste each other's time" indicate that he is sick of dating and probably frustrated that he has not yet found "the one." The phrase "ready to meet the one" can and should be taken literally. This gentleman is stating exactly what he wants: a serious relationship that ends in marriage. This guy wants a girlfriend badly and is almost a little desperate for one. He has thought a lot about this and is looking for a wife. I would venture that he wants to be married within a year. If a girl asked me if she should go out with this guy, I would make sure that she knew that he was looking for something very serious and probably wants to move pretty fast.

Profile 3:

I am a very easy going guy who likes to have fun. I really love dining at nice quiet out of the way restaurants. Even though I live in Washington DC, I really much prefer going out in Arlington or Fairfax VA. I just don't like the hustle and bustle of the city. I am very busy and travel all the time sometimes even on weekends which makes it very hard to find that special someone to connect with. I am looking for that special someone who wants a romantic partner who is ok with me not always being available. To be completely honest, I lead a very hectic work life. For this reason, I don't have very many friends to socialize with. I am a very private person with little drama in my life. I am ready to find you if you are ready to be found.

Let's look at those key phrases again:

- to have fun

- really love dining at nice quiet out of the way restaurants

- Even though I live in Washington DC, I really much prefer going out in Arlington or Fairfax VA

- very busy and travel all the time sometimes even on weekends

- ok with me not always being available. To be completely honest, I lead a very hectic work life.

- I don't have very many friends

- very private person

First off, he is looking to "have some fun," indicating that he might not be looking for something serious. That in itself might not be too telling, but when you put the whole thing together, it takes on a different meaning. There is no reason that a guy would actually bother stating that he "really" likes out of the way places and likes going out miles away from his home unless he didn't want you anywhere near his home. Also notice the use of the word "really," indicating that this is very important to him. He is "very busy and not always available, even on weekends." If someone were really that busy with work, they would merely state that work had been keeping them from meeting someone; they wouldn't need to go into detail about not being available on weekends. Again, it is important to him that you know that he is "very" busy. In Chapter 9, we learned a deceptive statement analysis technique in which a person uses qualifiers before a statement, indicating deception. Notice his use of "to be completely honest"; again, when someone insists that they are being completely honest, often the opposite is true. No one would bother saying that they don't have many friends because most people know that saying that makes them look bad—unless, of course, he wants to give you a reason as to why you will never meet any of his friends. He also has let you know that he is a "very private person," indicating that he does not want you to dig too deeply into his personal life. Again, by his use of the word "very," this is clearly very important to him. Do not walk away from this man, *run*.

If you are a really savvy lady, you might want to look this guy up on your Lulu app. I am sorry to say, ladies, but chances are high that this guy is married.

Even if you're not seeking a relationship, take some time to peruse dating sites to practice the skills that you have learned. See if you can tell who is telling the truth and who is being deceptive.

Detecting Deception in the After-the-Date Text Message

Now let's take a look at how to read deception in text messages after the first date. There are countless television shows and many books dedicated to trying to decipher what a man or woman means when he/she says that he/she will call after a date. I can't tell you how many times I have hung out with male and female friends as they re-read the same text, e-mail or Facebook message over and over again, trying to figure out whether the other person was interested or not, and what his or her intentions were. Today we often communicate with our love interests or work colleagues via text or e-mail, so we don't have the luxury of being able to read body language or vocal cues such as tone of voice or pitch. When you are trying to gauge interest from social media messages, e-mails, or text messages, instead of attempting to analyze the other person's intent, it is best to actually analyze the words. Remember, the truth almost always finds a way of leaking out, and people are actually very good at saying exactly what they think or feel. You just have to look at the words and see if any deception techniques are being used. For this book, I gathered some sample text messages from a single friend's conversations with potential love interests that she had received and sent during courtships. We will analyze them using the modified statement analysis techniques we already learned.

A female friend of mine went on what she thought was a great date. The man was charming and nice, and they had a lot of fun. She texted him the next day.

Her: "Did you make it home ok last night"

Him: "Had fun last night. Should get together again sometime. What are you up to?"

She saw his response as encouraging. However, if you look closely at the words, you will see that even though he probably did have fun, he most likely does not have any intention of seeing her again. First off, he does not put himself in the message (no "I" or "me"), showing that he might not be too invested. By using the word "should," he is not saying anything concrete and is being non-committal. He is giving himself an out. He does not indicate that he is going to call, nor does he make any plans as to when they will meet again. He may or may not call, but he is not committed to the relationship; probably, he's looking for someone he is more interested in but might keep her around as an option, just in case. He is using the distracting technique, trying to change the subject by asking her what she is up to.

If he wanted to see her again, his text would have stated his intentions clearly and read something like this:

Him: "Last night was fun. I would like to see you again. I'll call you after work."

In this text message, he puts himself in the message. He has clearly stated that he would like to see her again and has given a time when he wants to plan the next date.

The next example is a text message from a friend who went out on a date with a man who called her the next day. He told her that he was about to have the work week from hell because he had a proposal due, but would love to see her again at the end of the week. At the end of the week, she hadn't heard from him, so she sent him a text:

Her: "Haven't heard from you in a while. Want to meet up"
Him: "Been busy. Work stuff. How have you been?"

If you look at the actual words, you see that this is again most likely a blow-off. He may really have been busy with a work proposal. However, he asks how she is. He is using the "not answering the question" technique because he is deflecting the question. Instead of stating outright whether or not he wants to meet up, he asks how she is, again using the distraction technique. If he had been interested in seeing her again, he would have said something like this:

Him: "Work has been insane. Proposal due. Been pulling allnighters. Been thinking about you. Want to get dinner tomorrow night? Will be finished with proposal."

Here he says that he has been thinking about her and has been pulling all-nighters at work. He makes concrete plans to see her again. By simply reading the actual words and seeing what is there and what isn't, you can get a pretty good idea of what a potential date's e-mails or text messages are really telling you.

Now that you have a better understanding of how to read the real intentions behind the words, pay special attention to the social media, e-mail, and text message conversations that you have with others. By using the various techniques we learned here, you will be much more aware of and better able to detect potential deception.

Reading Deception in Advertisements

Most of us have used Craigslist or another free Website to purchase or sell something. We have to be very careful when using these sites because, often, the ads are deceptive. The following is taken from an ad for a car for sale that I found on one of these Websites:

"THIS CAR IS IN VERY VERY VERY GOOD CONDITION. NO PROBLEMS EVER. IT IS A STEAL. THIS CAR RAN GOOD."

Maybe English is not this person's first language. However, if you are doling out your hard-earned money on something, you should definitely not waste your time looking at this car. If you did, I would hope that you at least obtained a Carfax report on the car. You would most likely find that the car is actually not in VERY VERY VERY GOOD CONDITION. The all caps might just be a way that the seller is using to attempt to get a buyer's attention. By making definitive statement of "no problems ever," the seller is trying way too hard to convince the buyer. Also take note of the three "verys," implying that it is important to them that you believe this statement. I believe that you would find that this car has had many problems. The statement that the car "ran good" could just be bad grammar. Or, it could just be that the author is using the tense-hopping technique we discussed in Chapter 9. The author's use of a past-tense descriptor could mean that at one point, the car did run very well but doesn't anymore.

Take some time to practice your deception skills by looking at sellers' ads on Craigslist or eBay.

Reading Deception in the Job Seeker

If you work in HR or are involved in hiring, it is important to learn to read deception in resumes, cover letters, e-mails, text messages, and on posted social media content. You now have a good idea of what to look for using statement analysis, but let's practice a bit more. Look at the two examples of sentences from two cover letters and try to determine which one is true.

Example 1

I managed a team that successfully sold $1.7 million worth of X. Through my leadership, the team managed to win the coveted X company leadership award for 2012.

Example 2

Was part of a team that successfully sells millions worth of X. To be frank, I was definitely an integral part of the success of the company and won a major award.

If you picked Example 2 as the lie, you are correct. In the first sentence, the candidate changes from the past to the present tense. Example 2 also states an arbitrary number of "millions," which may or may not be true. Example 1 states an exact, rounded number. Example 2 uses the qualifying statement "to be frank," which is often an indication that this person is not being "frank." The descriptive use of "definitely" is the candidate's way of trying to prove to you that what he/she is saying is true. If it was true, this person would not need to use such unnecessary, descriptive filler words. Also notice that Example 1 mentions the exact name and year of the award, while Example 2 uses an arbitrary award.

– – –

Managing your online identity and learning to read deception can only work to your advantage. If you determine someone is not being truthful, adapting your response to the situation gives you the upper hand. More importantly, now that you are armed with modified statement analysis skills and the Catching the Catfisher Checklist, you can keep yourself and your children safe from liars, catfishers, and predators. How great is that?

Notes

Chapter 1

1. *www.theblaze.com/stories/2012/11/22/update-mass-women-fired-for-flipping-off-the-tomb-of-the-unknown-soldier/*.

2. *Social Media and the Law: A Guidebook for Communication Studies; Chapter 3, Privacy and Terms of Use* by Woodrow Hartzog, Cumberland School of Law—Stanford University.

3. Taken from Facebook Statement of Rights and Responsibilities. Date of last revision: December 11, 2012.

4. *www.foxnews.com/us/2013/06/23/student-launches-2m-lawsuit-against-school-district-over-facebook-photo/?test=latestnews#ixzz2X918ysSQ*.

5. *http://bostinno.streetwise.co/2012/11/21/lindsey-stone-fired-for-facebook-photo/*.

6. *www.law.cornell.edu/constitution/first_amendment*.

7. Taken from Chapter 1 of *Social Media and the Law: A Guidebook for Communication Studies* by Jennifer Jacobs Henderson, Trinity University.

8. "When Oversharing Online Can Get You Arrested" by Lauren Russell, CNN. Updated 8:59 a.m. EDT, Wednesday, April 24, 2013: *www.cnn.com/2013/04/18/tech/social-media/online-oversharing-arrests*.

Chapter 2

1. Facebook Data Use Policy Last updated December 11, 2012: *www.facebook.com/about/privacy*.

2. *http://mag.newsweek.com/2010/10/22/forget-privacy-what-the-internet-knows-about-you.html*. *Newsweek* magazine: "What the Internet Knows About You" (October 22, 2010).

3. *www.mozilla.org/en-GB/firefox/geolocation/*.

4. "Lettuce-Defiling Burger King Employee Tracked Down by 4chan Users, Terminated," by Neetzan Zimmerman. July 18, 2012, 10:08 a.m.: *http://gawker.com/5926982/lettuce+defiling-burger-king-employee-tracked-down-by-4chan-users-terminated*.

5. *"Super Cookies"—New Web Code Draws Concern Over Privacy Risks* by Tanzina Vega, eBrand Media Research Department, Oct. 11, 2010: *http://digitalarteries.com/advertising-marketing/marketing/super-cookies-new-web-code-draws-concern-over-privacy-risks/*.

6. *www.irfanview.com/.*

7. *http://support.mozilla.org/en-US/kb/private-brows-ing-browse-web-without-saving-info.*

8. *http://download.cnet.com/CCleaner/.*

Chapter 3

1. *http://pss.sagepub.com/content/17/7/592.abstract*

2. *http://money.cnn.com/2013/08/26/technology/social/facebook-credit-score/index.html?hpt=hp_t2. First published: August 26, 2013: 6:20 a.m. ET.*

Chapter 4

1. *www.tineye.com/.*

2. *www.google.com/insidesearch/features/images/search byimage.html.*

3. *http://articles.latimes.com/2013/mar/11/science/la-sci-facebook-likes-20130312.*

Chapter 5

1. *Time* magazine, "How Recruiters Use Social Networks to Make Hiring Decisions Now" by Dan Schawbel, July 9, 2012: *http://business.time.com/2012/07/09/how-recruiters-use-social-networks-to-make-hiring-decisions-now/.*

2. Ibid.

3. *http://m.npr.org/news/Science/171975368.*

4. *http://gobefore.me/.*

5. *https://onlulu.com/.*

Chapter 6

1. *www.match.com/*.

2. *www.eharmony.com/*.

3. *www.jdate.com/*.

4. *www.christianmingle.com/*.

Chapter 7

1. *www.statisticbrain.com/cyber-bullying-statistics/*.

2. *www.tylerclementi.org/tylers-story/*.

3. *http://en.wikipedia.org/wiki/Suicide_of_Audrie_Pott*.

4. *http://en.wikipedia.org/wiki/Suicide_of_Rehtaeh_Parsons*.

5. *www.todaystmj4.com/features/specialassignment/95355134.html*.

6. From *Social Media and Law*.

7. *http://stopcyberbullying.org/prevention/schools_role.html*.

8. *www.sheriff.org/faqs/displayfaq.cfm?id=ba787291-0b05-4ab2-9840-b9697bba4cce*

9. *https://chrome.google.com/webstore/detail/webpage-screenshot-capture/ckibcdccnfeookdmbahgiakhnjcd-dpki*.

10. *www.telestream.net/screenflow/*.

Chapter 8

1. *http://en.wikipedia.org/wiki/ScottThompson_%28bus inessman%29.*

2. *http://deadspin.com/manti-teos-dead-girlfriend-the-most-heartbreaking-an-5976517.*

3. *w w w . n y t i m e s . c o m / 2 0 1 1 / 0 6 / 1 3 / worldmiddleeast/13blogger.html?_r=0.*

4. *http://techland.time.com/2011/08/03/report-92-of-newt-gingrichs-twitter-followers-arent-real/.*

5. *www.theguardian.com/world/2013/sep/23/new-york-fake-online-reviews-yoghurt.*

6. *www.bbb.org/.*

Chapter 9

1. *10 Easy Ways to Spot a Liar: The Best Techniques of Statement Analysis, Nonverbal Communication and Handwriting Analysis*, by Mark McClish.

Chapter 10

1. *www.mtv.com/shows/catfish/series.jhtml.*

2. Vince Pierce in Catfish documentary film directed by Henry Joost and Ariel Schulman: *www.iamrogue .com/catfish.*

3. *http://en.wikipedia.org/wiki/Suicide_of_Megan_Meier.*

4. Networkworld.com article, "The Robin Sage experiment: Fake profile fools security pros, an experiment that called for creating a fake social networking personality managed to snare even seasoned security veterans," by Joan Goodchild, CSO, July 8, 2010: *www.networkworld.com/news/2010/070810-the-robin-sage-experiment-fake.html.*

Index

G

H

I

J

K

R

S

About the Author

Tyler Cohen Wood is cyber branch chief for an Intelligence agency within the Department of Defense (DoD) where she makes decisions and recommendations significantly changing, interpreting, and developing important cyber policies and programs affecting current and future DoD and Intelligence policies. She is well known in the Intelligence, DoD, law enforcement, and computer forensics communities for her work with digital forensics and cyber intelligence.

Tyler has presented as a cyber expert at conferences across the country. She coauthored the textbook *Alternate Data Storage Forensics* and was featured in *Best Damn Cybercrime and Digital Forensics Book Period.*

Prior to joining the Agency, she worked for the DoD Cyber Crime Center (DC3) as a senior digital forensic analyst, using her expertise in intrusion, malware analysis, and major crimes to achieve many successful prosecutions and saving the commercial industry millions of dollars. Before joining DC3, she was employed at IBM and NASA as a senior forensic analyst, where she also showcased her expertise in intrusions and major crimes.